BUILDING A LEGACY

THE RESTORATION OF FRANK LLOYD WRIGHT'S OAK PARK HOME AND STUDIO

EDITED BY ZARINE WEIL

FRANK LLOYD WRIGHT PRESERVATION TRUST

Pomegranate

SAN FRANCISCO

Published by Pomegranate Communications, Inc.

Box 6099, Rohnert Park, California 94927

800 277 1428; www.pomegranate.com

Pomegranate Europe Ltd.

Fullbridge House, Fullbridge

Maldon, Essex CM9 4LE, England

Library of Congress Cataloging-in-Publication Data

Building a legacy : the restoration of Frank Lloyd Wright's Oak Park Home and Studio / the Frank Lloyd Wright Preservation Trust.
     p. cm.
  Includes bibliographical references.
  ISBN 0-7649-1461-8 (alk. paper)
    1. Frank Lloyd Wright House (Oak Park, Ill.) 2. Frank Lloyd Wright Studio (Oak Park, Ill.) 3. Wright, Frank Lloyd, 1867-1959—Homes and haunts—Illinois—Oak Park.4. Architecture, Domestic—Conservation and restoration—Illinois—Oak Park. 5. Prairie school (Architecture)—Illinois—Oak Park. 6. Oak Park (Ill.)—Buildings, structures, etc. I. Frank Lloyd Wright Preservation Trust.

NA7238.028 B85 2001
728'.37'092—dc21

00-063675

Pomegranate Catalog No. A592

Cover and book design by Lynn Bell, Monroe Street Studios.

Printed in Korea

09 08 07 06 05 04 03 02 01   10 9 8 7 6 5 4 3 2 1

CONTENTS

FOREWORD

As the Frank Lloyd Wright Preservation Trust commemorates in print the story of its restoration of Frank Lloyd Wright's first home and studio, my participation as a member of the Wright family and as an architect invite reflection. I am led to ponder what architecture and these buildings have meant to my family, and also the emotions that both we and members of the Trust brought to the Home and Studio's restoration.

It is no secret that architecture has been a driving force for my family for well over a century. The all-consuming passion that my grandfather, Frank Lloyd Wright, felt for architecture is legendary. No one who met him even once—or has seen even one of his buildings—could doubt that for an instant.

Much of my grandfather's work was directed to answering one question: How can I improve the life of the average American family and make it more beautiful? He began considering that question as a young man while he lived and worked in Oak Park, and he remained devoted to answering it through the end of his life at age ninety-one. The ideal of the family always remained dear to him—perhaps more so than the reality.

Just as the idea of family was a constant thread in my grandfather's architecture, so too has architecture profoundly shaped the lives of my family members down through the decades, starting with my father, Lloyd Wright (Frank Lloyd Wright's oldest child and a gifted architect in his own right).

Dad lived at the home on Forest Avenue until he was nineteen and then left to attend the University of Wisconsin. His stories of his Oak Park childhood made a great impact on me as a child because it was largely through them that I came to know my grandfather, grandmother, aunts and uncles in this period of my grandfather's life. My father always remembered the wonderful parties my grandfather loved to have. Two or three times a week my grandparents would invite friends over from Chicago or the Oak Park area. One of the things my father remembered best was the Christmas Eve parties. There was always a huge Christmas tree in the playroom, just as the Trust has now each holiday season.

My grandfather loved to collect Persian carpets. He would go to auctions in Chicago and come back with bales of Persian rugs that were collected right from the floors of Persia. My father would have to beat them, wash them and then hang them up to dry. He was fascinated by all the patterns on the carpets. Those are the rugs that show up in all the early photographs of the house. My grandfather was also one of the great collectors of Japanese prints. My father remembered Grandfather coming home with new prints. They would take them into the studio, and Grandfather would demonstrate how to make mounts for the prints while he talked about them: their wonderful proportions, abstract qualities and two-dimensional aspects. Dad always considered these times to be wonderful learning experiences.

My father was also a talented draftsman. Grandfather had him working in the office when he was about fifteen. Dad became an absolutely superb renderer. He worked in tempera and carbon pencil, a technique he learned from the great renderer Marion Mahony (who worked in the Oak Park Studio). I remember my grandfather saying that he considered my father to be one of the great architectural renderers. My grandfather always kept Dad's rendering of the San Marcos Hotel above his desk. One day,

Grandfather pointed to it and said to me, "That's the best work your father has ever done." I thought, wait a minute—what about all the buildings he has designed? Oh, well—Dad did get quite a bit of experience.

I also got my start in architecture when I was fifteen. I went to work with Grandfather on his farm at Taliesin. Before then, I had planned to study animal husbandry at college, but the creative energy at Taliesin made me realize I loved architecture even more than animals.

At Taliesin I felt more like an apprentice than a grandson, yet I was closer to Grandfather than ever before. I understood him more than I ever had as "just" a grandchild. During my childhood I had known him through sporadic visits to Taliesin East or West or his visits once or twice a year to my parents' home in Los Angeles. We did not have a continuous relationship until I got to the Fellowship.

Since I was a beginning apprentice, I did not have much contact with my grandfather, unlike the senior apprentices. But he was very good about coming into the drafting room and sitting down with all the younger apprentices—not just me—to see what we were working on and how we were getting along.

The one form of special treatment I received is that my grandfather and my grandmother, Olgivanna, always invited me over for dinner a couple of times each week. Grandfather typically ate breakfast and lunch with the Fellowship in the dining room, followed by a private dinner in the main house. It was a delightful treat for me to spend the evening with them, but they actually thought I preferred to spend my time with the apprentices.

The life of an apprentice at Taliesin was a magnificent mélange of drafting, construction, waiting on tables, cooking, decorating the theater, taking care of the animals and garden, poetry, and music, with chorus and ensemble, for Sunday evening performances by the apprentices. All this magnificent energy swirled around with my grandfather and grandmother at the center.

And that was how I got my start in architecture, as Grandfather's legacy continued into the third generation. During my fifty years in the pursuit of organic architecture, I have incorporated the teachings of my grandfather and father into my work every time I pick up a pencil. I don't worry about comparisons. My grandfather and I are two different people. He was one in a century—and in architecture, one in a millennium.

There is no question in my mind that, of all my grandfather's buildings that have been restored, the Home and Studio has received the finest restoration. What makes this restoration so special is the affection and energy of all the people involved. To my knowledge, none of his other buildings—wonderful creations all—have had this amount of care and have been loved so deeply by so many people.

Many thousands of hours of work were donated by volunteers, in addition to the hours put in by highly skilled hired construction crews and staff. This amazing outpouring imbues the complex with a special spirit that could not be there otherwise, even with my grandfather's genius. Even now, over a decade since the restoration's completion, more than five hundred volunteers continue to donate thousands of hours to the Trust each year.

Just as these buildings have inspired passion among those directly responsible for their restoration and ongoing care, the restoration process stirred strong feelings in my family as well. I remember when my father received the phone call telling him that the Trust, then in its infancy, had acquired the property and was preparing to begin restoration. "This is wonderful news!" he told me, having visited the subdivided and much-altered property before its restoration and been dismayed to see that so little of his childhood home remained visible through its various "modernizations."

From there, the whole Wright family got involved, including my uncle David and my cousins, Anne Baxter and Elizabeth Wright Ingraham (yet another gifted architect). It was especially wonderful—and vital to the restoration—to hear my father and Uncle David discuss their childhood memories. They both had vivid recall and knew exactly how every feature of the building should look—or so they thought. Unfortunately, their memories did not always mesh! The fact that John Thorpe, Bill Dring, Don Kalec and the rest of the restoration committee were able to reconcile their sometimes-conflicting reminiscences, while dealing tactfully with both men, has always impressed me.

Pointing out that there were some legitimate differences of opinion about the restoration does nothing to minimize the Trust's accomplishment. If anything, these differences reveal just how massive an undertaking the restoration really was. For instance, I have overseen the restoration of several of my grandfather's buildings in southern California, as well as Auldbrass Plantation in South Carolina (1939), and can honestly say that I view restoration a little differently than a true restoration architect or preservationist does. What I try to do is consider the effect that I believe my grandfather desired. I will often find, in my grandfather's working drawings, details that were not executed or materials not used because of cost. I will go back to these original details in the restoration even if the building was not built that way.

In Oak Park, however, the guiding principle for the restoration was always to re-create what my grandfather actually built, not what he may have wished to build. Thus, the stork capitals outside the Studio were recast in plaster to be just as the originals were. I strongly believe that my grandfather cast them in plaster only because he could not afford to cast them in bronze, so I wanted the Trust to cast the reproductions in bronze.

This same adherence to a clearly stated restoration objective—returning the property to its 1909 appearance, the last year my grandfather lived and worked there—also caused a bit of temporary strife between my father and the Trust. My father's firm opinion was that a 1911 cantilever over the studio entrance should be left on because it had been added by my grandfather and not by some later, lesser light. And the cantilever, of course, is one of the most important statements that my grandfather made during his entire seven decades in architecture. In the end, the Trust decided to remove the cantilever for the sake of consistency. My father realized that selecting the exact restoration date was a hard call, and peace was eventually restored.

These instances reveal both the mettle of spirit and depth of feelings the Trust board members had for the Home and Studio. It would have undoubtedly been easier, and entirely understandable, to acquiesce to the great man's son and grandson. Yet the Trust remained true to its vision. There is much to admire in such resolve.

However, the Trust's more recent acquisition and ongoing restoration of one of my grandfather's true masterpieces, the house he designed for Frederick C. Robie in Chicago's Hyde Park neighborhood, is indeed wonderful news. In a sense, this restoration will actually close the circle begun in 1974. The Robie House (1910)—created by my grandfather from his Oak Park home and studio—contains the very essence of the Prairie home, not the least of which are those world-famous cantilevers. Somehow, I think the aptness of this must not be lost on Dad, although he has been gone since 1978.

Finally, I would like to thank the Frank Lloyd Wright Preservation Trust and all its volunteers, past and present. Their accomplishments have been truly remarkable. Speaking not only for myself but also as a member of the Wright family, we appreciate so much what they have done. There have been hundreds of them, and that translates into tens of thousands of hours that have been put into this organization over the past twenty-five years. They are as much a part of the buildings as the Wrights are, and the buildings are as much their home as ours.

This book is a documentation of the Home and Studio's restoration process and everything that went into it—the technical decisions as well as the human equation of the restoration. It offers a welcome opportunity to consider why my grandfather made the decisions he did about the Home and Studio's design and construction and also how the property embodies his lifelong quest to create organic architecture.

Perusing its pages makes me eagerly anticipate the discoveries that lie ahead as the Frank Lloyd Wright Preservation Trust turns its attention to restoring the Robie House. My hope for the Trust is that, in a few years, I will be asked to pen the foreword to a similar book that documents the Robie House's restoration!

—Eric Lloyd Wright, architect
Los Angeles, California, June 2000

PREFACE AND ACKNOWLEDGMENTS

On its twenty-fifth anniversary in 1999, the Frank Lloyd Wright Preservation Trust, then known as the Frank Lloyd Wright Home and Studio Foundation, explored the idea of celebrating this milestone with a small commemorative booklet. As we researched our organizational history, the story that emerged had multiple themes. On one level, it was about an incredibly successful grassroots effort at historic preservation. On another, it was about the revitalization of a community. It was also about the altruistic spirit in hundreds of individuals drawn together by a historic building they were determined to save. Unifying these themes was the restoration itself: a thirteen-year award-winning effort to preserve when possible and re-create when necessary the early home and workplace of one of America's greatest architects.

Hundreds of pages and thousands of images recording the restoration are in the Frank Lloyd Wright Preservation Trust's Research Center. However, the restoration had never been comprehensively documented in one place. The time seemed right to do just that, and so the planned booklet grew into a book-length work.

This book is an account of the technical decisions and human elements that comprised the restoration process. It covers the history and significance of the buildings, the Oak Park community's role in the preservation effort, restoration philosophy and methodologies, and the actual work performed. Although it tries to respect the time sequence of events and provides in-depth information, its guiding principles are clarity over chronology and accessibility rather than a high degree of specialization. Those interested in historic preservation or Frank Lloyd Wright, or both, should find the book a fitting and valuable commemoration.

Many talented people contributed to *Building a Legacy*. Special thanks are due to: Joan B. Mercuri, for supporting the project; Don Kalec and John Thorpe, for being so generous with immense quantities of knowledge, hard-to-find images and editorial comments that greatly enriched the text; Cheryl Bachand and Karen Sweeney, for making suggestions on numerous drafts and tutoring the uninitiated in architectural matters; Jack Lesniak, for reviewing the manuscript; Ross Elfline, for being ever-willing to look up the research question of the day; Jennifer Gray, for digging out dozens of slides from the archives; Darcy Lewis, Karla Kaulfuss and Jack Woodhull, for their smart editing; Erin Janulis, for pulling together any loose strands as we neared the deadline for the manuscript; Rosemarie Larry, for helping with a variety of tasks; Michael Houlahan of Hedrich Blessing Photographers, for his generosity with the images of the Home and Studio; Oscar Munoz of The Frank Lloyd Wright Foundation, and Angela Giral of the Avery Architectural and Fine Arts Library, Columbia University, for permitting the use of historic photographs; Frank Lloyd Wright's architect grandchildren, Eric Lloyd Wright and Elizabeth Wright Ingraham, for contributing the foreword and afterword; Dawn Goshorn Schumann, for sharing her files on the early days of the organization; Carol Kelm, Fran Martone and Audra Bellmore, for their painstakingly researched writing; Jeanette Fields, for her account of the Oak Park Tour Center; and finally, Katie Burke and Eva Strock of Pomegranate Communications, Inc., as well as Lynn Bell of Monroe Street Studios, for bringing this work to life.

—Zarine Weil

In September 2000, the Frank Lloyd Wright Home and Studio Foundation adopted a new name, Frank Lloyd Wright Preservation Trust, to reflect its stewardship of two museum sites, the Oak Park Home and Studio as well as Wright's Frederick C. Robie House on the University of Chicago campus. When referring to the time frame of the restoration, 1974–1987, the text uses the name by which the organization was known then.

CONTRIBUTORS

Cheryl Bachand is the curator at the Frank Lloyd Wright Preservation Trust and an adjunct faculty member in art history and museum studies at Barat College, Lake Forest, Illinois.

Audra Bellmore is the archivist and librarian at the Research Center of the Frank Lloyd Wright Preservation Trust.

Donald Kalec is a professor of interior architecture/historic preservation at the School of the Art Institute of Chicago, an architect, and former Taliesin Fellow. He is a twenty-seven-year volunteer at the Frank Lloyd Wright Preservation Trust and served as director of research and restoration during the restoration of the Oak Park Home and Studio.

Carol Kelm has been a volunteer at the Frank Lloyd Wright Preservation Trust for twenty-two years. She has served as an interpreter and as a member of the collections committee as well as the public programs council. She is actively involved with a variety of historic preservation organizations.

Darcy Lewis is an award-winning freelance writer in Riverside, Illinois, and a twelve-year volunteer at the Frank Lloyd Wright Preservation Trust. She has written about architecture-related topics for the *Chicago Tribune* and other newspapers and was the project coordinator for *AIA Guide to Chicago*.

Fran Martone is the author of *In Wright's Shadow: Artists and Architects in the Oak Park Studio*. She is also a professional actress, performing regularly in the Chicago area.

Karen Sweeney AIA is the director of restoration at the Frank Lloyd Wright Preservation Trust and an architect. She was closely involved in the Oak Park Home and Studio's restoration, serving as vice chairperson of the restoration committee.

John G. Thorpe AIA played a key role in the restoration of the Oak Park Home and Studio. He was a chairperson of the restoration committee and has been a volunteer at the Frank Lloyd Wright Preservation Trust for twenty-seven years. His firm, John G. Thorpe & Associates, specializes in the restoration of Frank Lloyd Wright and other Prairie-style houses.

Zarine Weil is the publications manager at the Frank Lloyd Wright Preservation Trust as well as a freelance writer and editor.

Frank Lloyd Wright on the veranda of his Oak Park home, c. 1890–1910. Photograph: Frank Lloyd Wright Foundation, Scottsdale, Arizona.

*. . . **A**n entirely new sense of architecture . . . had emerged. A higher concept of architecture. . . . architecture for the spirit of man, for life as life must be lived today; architecture spiritually (virtually) conceived as appropriate enclosure of interior space to be lived in. Form and function made one. The enclosed space within them is the reality of the building.*

—Frank Lloyd Wright
"Organic Architecture,"
Architects' Journal, August 1936

Frank Lloyd Wright's first home and studio is a unique structure in the history of world architecture for three reasons.

First, it was an intimate creation by one of the world's greatest architects for himself and his family. Few architects throughout history have lived or worked in buildings they designed. Wright was unique in that he created, over his lifetime, nine homes and workshops for himself—only three of which are still in existence. Wright obviously believed that his environment was of prime importance, not only for visual delight, but—more importantly—as a stimulus for creative work.

Second, Wright's personal spaces were palettes upon which he experimented with materials, forms, colors and even the shaping of space itself. His own homes were "charcoal sketches" to be erased and rebuilt as he gained new insights into the art of architecture. Thus, Wright's Oak Park Home and Studio is a twenty-year tracing of his development of the Prairie style of architecture—experiments and models, beginnings and endings, successes and failures. Few other architects have had the patience, energy and drive to subject themselves to the chaos of constant remodeling, even in the quest of a personal vision.

Third, the combining of home and workplace was (and still is) a common way of life for artists, but not usually for American architects; the only precedent was H. H. Richardson, and that was due to illness. Midway through his Oak Park years Wright added his studio to his home, establishing an integrated environment he continued in his final two homes, Taliesin and Taliesin West.

West façade of the Home, c. 1890–95. Photographer unknown. Published in H. R. Hitchcock, In the Nature of Materials, *1942. Photograph: Frank Lloyd Wright Preservation Trust.*

Frank Lloyd Wright's very first house design—he was twenty-two at the time—was a small home for himself and his bride, Catherine. It was financed by Wright's employer and mentor, Louis Sullivan, and built on a wooded lot at the corner of Chicago and Forest Avenues in Oak Park, Illinois.

For the design of his home, Wright borrowed from the Shingle- and Cottage-style homes he would have seen in *Architectural News and Building Report* and in pattern books of the late 1800s. From the Cottage style, Wright took the near-symmetrical façade and the simple, straightforward plan. From the Shingle style, he used the high-pitched gable roof with

Frank Lloyd Wright was born in 1867 in Richland Center, Wisconsin. His father, William Carey Wright, was a minister and a music master whose many short-lived pastoral assignments took his family to parishes in Iowa, Rhode Island and Massachusetts when Frank was a child. His mother, Anna Lloyd Wright, was a strong-willed woman who, according to Wright's auto-biography, was determined that her first-born would be an architect. She introduced her son to the Froebel "gifts"—a system of teaching form and geometry through sets of wooden blocks, strips of paper, beads, string and sticks. Later Wright stated, "I soon became susceptible to constructive pattern evolving in everything I saw. I learned to 'see' this way and when I did, I did not care to draw casual incidentals of Nature. I wanted to design." (*A Testament,* 1957)

In 1878 the family returned to Wisconsin, where Wright attended public schools in Madison. In 1887, after two semesters of engineering at the University of Wisconsin, he dropped out of college and set out for Chicago to seek a career in architecture.

Wright's first employer was Joseph Lyman Silsbee, who had built a repu-tation for picturesque Shingle-style residences—a style that Wright followed in his own Oak Park home. At his next job, with the architecture firm of Adler & Sullivan, Wright was deeply influenced by the ideas and work of Louis Sullivan, who became his mentor. From Sullivan, Wright learned about deco-rative designs based on nature and grew familiar with the principle that form should follow function. Hired to develop detailed sketches for the Auditorium Building (Chicago, 1889), Wright was soon promoted to head draftsman.

In 1893, after Sullivan discovered that Wright was violating his contract with his employers by taking on commissions of his own, the two men had a parting of ways, and Wright opened his own office at the Schiller Building in Chicago.

Frank Lloyd Wright, c. 1904–06. Photograph: Frank Lloyd Wright Preservation Trust.

Five years later he expanded his architectural practice to Oak Park, where he built a studio addition to his home. In 1909 Wright left his family and Oak Park for Berlin, Germany, with Mamah Borthwick Cheney, the wife of a client. There the publication of *Ausgeführte Bauten und Entwürfe von Frank Lloyd Wright* (also known as the Wasmuth Portfolio) a retrospective of his Prairie-style work, brought him international renown. In 1910 he returned briefly to Oak Park to convert his home into rental space for his family and to remodel his studio into a residence for them. He and Mrs. Cheney moved to Spring Green, Wisconsin, where Wright built his new home and workplace, Taliesin. ■

cross gables; the simple, unbroken exterior envelope; the use of wood shingles to cover both walls and roof; and the wide-arched openings between the major rooms on the ground floor. Integrating these elements, Wright added new ingredients to the mix as well. From his Froebel-block training, Wright used basic geometric shapes to structure both the massing and the details: triangular gables, diamond-paned windows, rectangular window and door openings, semicircular lunette windows and veranda bays. This was done with a crispness and precision not seen before in the Shingle style. While at Adler & Sullivan, Wright had learned how to design a super-efficient plan, one with little wasted space and a geometrical clarity not usually seen in small houses. The integration of these disparate elements into a whole new synthesis was Wright's genius. He was certainly not the first Midwestern architect to use the Shingle style, but he was the first to raise it to the level of serious architecture.

Oak Park was a bucolic village with a population of about four thousand in 1888, when Frank Lloyd Wright, his mother (Anna) and his sisters (Maginel and Jane) came to live in a red-brick house on Forest Avenue across the street from the estate of John Austin, real estate developer of Oak Park, Austin and River Forest. Historic photographs show giant oaks and elms arching over the unpaved side streets lined with brand-new suburban residences in the latest Victorian styles. Forest Avenue ended, to the north, at a dirt tract presumptuously named Chicago Avenue. Beyond was untouched prairie. While most of the first block of Forest Avenue north of Lake Street (the Main Street of Oak Park) already was filled with houses and a church, the second block north was still being developed. On the southeast corner of Forest and Chicago was an 88.3 X 165-foot lot and house that had belonged to a landscape gardener, John Blair. He and his family had

moved to British Columbia in search of opportunity, leaving the property to be sold by John Austin, Wright's neighbor.

The year 1889 was important for Wright. On June 1, the twenty-one-year-old Wright married eighteen-year-old Catherine Tobin of Chicago. The young couple lived temporarily with Wright's mother and sisters in a small Gothic Revival cottage that stood on John Blair's untended lot with its exotic plantings. Wright appealed to Louis Sullivan for a loan to buy the property (jointly with his mother) and build a small cottage for himself and his bride. Sullivan loaned him $5,000, to be deducted from his paycheck. The new house would face Forest Avenue (as was typical for Oak Park corner lots), leaving Anna's house at the east end of the lot, facing Chicago Avenue. ■

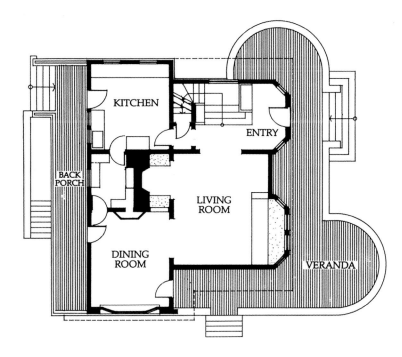

■ 1889 FIRST-FLOOR PLAN

The 1889 first-floor plan of the Home is simple and compact, with the living room and entry hall in the front of the house and the dining room, pantry and kitchen along the back. The rooms are grouped around a central fireplace, and receive light and air from at least two sides. This cruciform plan later became the basic layout of Wright's Prairie and Usonian houses. The openings between the entry, living room and dining room are wide, with no doors, creating an open spaciousness that belies the modest size of the house.

■ 1889 SECOND-FLOOR PLAN

The 1889 second-floor plan is also compact, with all the rooms opening onto a small central stair hall. Wright used a large room across the front as his studio for late-night work. On the east side, two closets and part of the bath overhang the back porch to gain living space. The master bedroom faces north and has a small balcony. The nursery faces south. The bath, closet and hallway act as sound barriers between the main rooms.

1895 DINING ROOM AND PLAYROOM ADDITION

■ 1895 FIRST-FLOOR PLAN

The 1895 first-floor plan shows the additions to the Home that were made to accommodate Wright's growing family. In thirteen years, the Wrights had six children: Lloyd was born in 1890, John in 1892, Catherine in 1894, David in 1895, Frances in 1898 and Llewellyn in 1903. Wright added a larger dining room where the kitchen used to be, and a service wing to the rear with a kitchen, maid's room and back stairs to the second floor. The former dining room became the family's study. He enlarged the living room by adding a second bay window to the north. The two bays met at the corner to create a large, wraparound window.

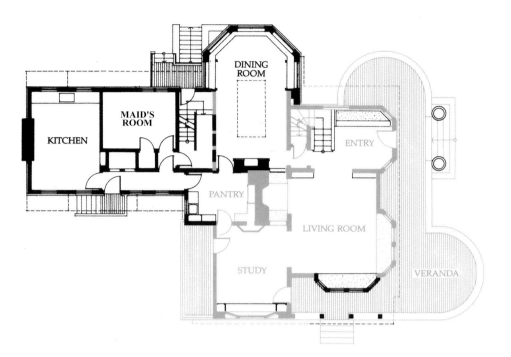

Key for floor plans:
Gray—Existing structure
Black—Sections that were added or changed.

■ 1895 SECOND-FLOOR PLAN

Upstairs, the 1895 addition consisted of a playroom for the children, located over the service area and accessed by the back stairs. Light was filtered through a skylight. On the north and south sides, bay windows with built-in window seats projected out from the walls.

At the same time, Wright divided his studio (along the west façade) in half with a seven-foot partition to make a bedroom on the south for the two girls and one on the north for the two boys. To the former nursery he added a large polygonal bay (directly over the dining room extension below). The room now became Catherine's dayroom.

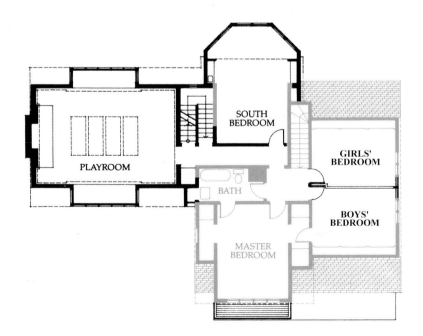

This 1906–07 photograph of the Studio shows the Chicago Avenue façade with the octagonal drum of the drafting room to the left and the octagonal library to the right. In the center is the entrance loggia. Photograph: Historical Society of Oak Park and River Forest. Published in Oak Park, Illinois, Bellman Association, Chicago, 1907.

1898 STUDIO ADDITION AND 1898–1909 ALTERATIONS

Weary of commuting to his downtown Chicago office and desiring to bring his work and family lives closer, Frank Lloyd Wright built a studio addition to his home in 1898.

The Studio represents the first time Wright began to explore the idea of innovative structure as opposed to conventional construction. Built of the same cedar shingles, common brick and wood trim as the Home, the Studio was visually integrated with the Home, yet its bold, asymmetrical grouping of geometric forms made a statement, just as Wright intended. The hollow two-story cubical/octagonal mass of the drafting room (on the left) was balanced and softly echoed by the story-and-a-half octagonal library (on the right). The lower entrance hall, making a solid masonry anchor in the middle, proclaimed its easy access by the openings in its loggia across the front, even though the entrance doors could not be seen.

The monumental octagonal drum of the drafting room appeared informed by discoveries ten to fifteen years earlier of pre-Columbian ruins in Central and South America. The Boulder sculptures and the plaster stork panels decorating the entrance represented a new American symbolism. The Studio was a built advertisement for Wright's architectural philosophy.

The outside shapes reflected the spaces of the rooms within. Exterior form and interior space became a unified entity—one of Wright's design principles. Similarly, the building was one with its site: foliage in urns and parkway planting beds incorporated the structure into its wooded setting of sheltering ginkgo and willow trees.

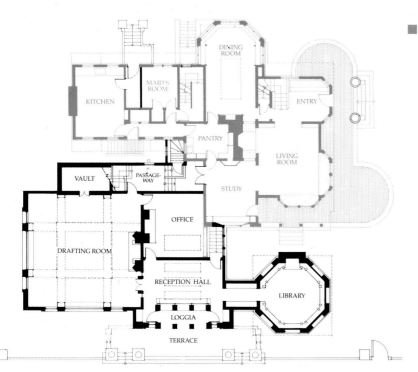

■ 1898–1909 FIRST-FLOOR PLAN

The Studio's business entrance was on Chicago Avenue. The building had a binuclear plan in which a central entrance led to areas on two sides. The reception hall had angled rear walls, with doorways leading to the drafting room on one side and to Wright's office on the other.

The large square drafting room had a masonry vault on one side for storing architectural drawings and Wright's Japanese print collection. On the west wall was an arched fireplace (backed up to a similar fireplace in Wright's office). A short hall separated the rest of the Studio from the library, the octagonal shape of which repeated the octagons of the Home's living room bay and the upper level of the drafting room. A passageway connected the Studio to the Home study. This passageway was famous for its design, which allowed the branches of a sprawling willow tree to grow right through the ceiling.

Between 1898 and 1909, Wright made several interior and exterior changes to the Studio. A low wall was built at the entrance to create a barrier from Chicago Avenue. In the reception hall, the angled rear walls were removed, making the room a larger rectangle.

■ 1898–1909 SECOND-FLOOR PLAN

The octagonal upper part of the drafting room housed a balcony. The balcony was used for sculptural work by Richard Bock (who collaborated with Wright on several projects), by Wright's sister Maginel as an artist's studio, and for amateur art-glass assembly by the drafting staff. The balcony was accessed by a narrow stair from the passageway below through the upper part of the vault. In the space above the vault, Wright had a photographic darkroom.

Between 1898 and 1909, both the drafting room and octagonal library received an additional band of clerestory windows above the existing window set. Weather skylights were added on the roof and art-glass panels to the ceilings of the reception hall and office to allow natural light to filter through and brighten the rooms. A weather skylight was also added over the octagonal library. Light filtered through panels of frosted glass in a suspended ceiling.

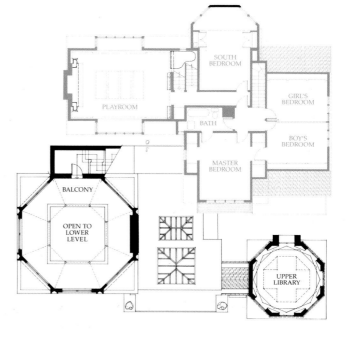

Frank Lloyd Wright's definition of an indigenous architecture evolved during his Oak Park years. He identified himself as a Midwesterner and found inspiration in the prairie landscape. "The prairie has a beauty of its own and we should recognize and accentuate this natural beauty, its quiet level. Hence, gently sloping roofs, low proportions, quiet sky lines, suppressed heavy-set chimneys and sheltering overhangs, low terraces and out-reaching walls sequestering private gardens," he wrote in 1908. ("In the Cause of Architecture," *Frank Lloyd Wright on Architecture: Selected Writings, 1894–1940)*

Although the Home and Studio are pre-Prairie style buildings, they contain the seeds of Wright's architectural philosophy. In his own living and working quarters, Wright experimented with principles that found their fullest expression in buildings that were designed in the Studio—masterpieces such as the Ward Willits House (Highland Park, Illinois, 1902), Susan Dana House (Springfield, Illinois, 1904), Darwin Martin House (Buffalo, New York, 1906), Meyer May House (Grand Rapids, Michigan, 1910), Unity Temple (Oak Park, Illinois, 1908) and Frederick C. Robie House (Chicago, 1910).

Characteristics of the Prairie style that Wright tested in his first home include a harmonious relationship between the building and its site; use of natural materials and earth-toned colors; a strong masonry base to anchor the building to the ground; geometric roof lines; the extension of interior spaces to terraces through banks of windows or glazed doors; an open floor plan with rooms flowing easily into one another; horizontal bands of casement windows, often with abstractions of natural patterns; a central, simply designed hearth; built-in furniture; furniture and decorative arts integrated with architecture to create a unified environment; the integration of heating and lighting with architecture; and wood banding to emphasize the horizontal line.

In his studio, Wright utilized principles that later characterized many of his public buildings: large, geometric masses interrupted by carefully placed openings; an indirect entry; a binuclear plan; a low, dark entry leading to a double-height space lit by skylights or clerestory windows; the free flow of vertical and horizontal space; heating and lighting integrated into the architecture or as decorative elements; the use of unique structural systems; and an intangible atmosphere of inspiration.

Wright did not approach design armed only with a static array of architectural principles. Rather, he always viewed his buildings with a fresh eye, unafraid to modify them in order to give shape to his ever-evolving vision. Early in his career, his home and workplace provided an ideal testing ground for the principles of the Prairie style of architecture—he could alter designs and plans whenever the need or desire arose. ■

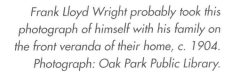

Frank Lloyd Wright probably took this photograph of himself with his family on the front veranda of their home, c. 1904. Photograph: Oak Park Public Library.

Catherine Wright seated in a hammock on the Home's veranda, n. d. Photograph: Frank Lloyd Wright Preservation Trust.

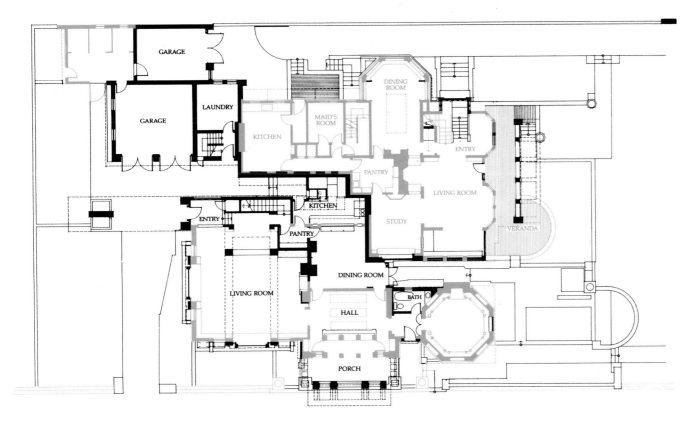

In the Home, a roof was added over the front veranda, the front door was moved to the south side as an added automobile entrance, and the living room was extended to the northern end of the veranda. Three garages and two concrete drives were added east of the Home.

A brick firewall was added between the Home and Studio, separating them completely so that there was no longer any connection between them.

In the Studio, the drafting room became a living room, Wright's office was converted into a dining room and the passageway became a kitchen. A walled garden was added to the west of the new dining room to offer private exterior space. A new bathroom was added in the exterior space between the octagonal library and the reception hall. The Chicago Avenue Studio entrance was walled in as a private outdoor porch with a sheltering roof and trellis. The front door to the Studio dwelling was moved to the southeast corner of the former drafting room, off the two new driveways serving the new garages.

1911 ALTERATIONS TO THE HOME AND STUDIO

■ 1911 FIRST-FLOOR PLAN

When Wright left Oak Park for Wisconsin in 1911, he converted the Home into a rental unit to provide income for his family. The Studio became the family's living quarters. These changes in the buildings' functions resulted in numerous structural modifications.

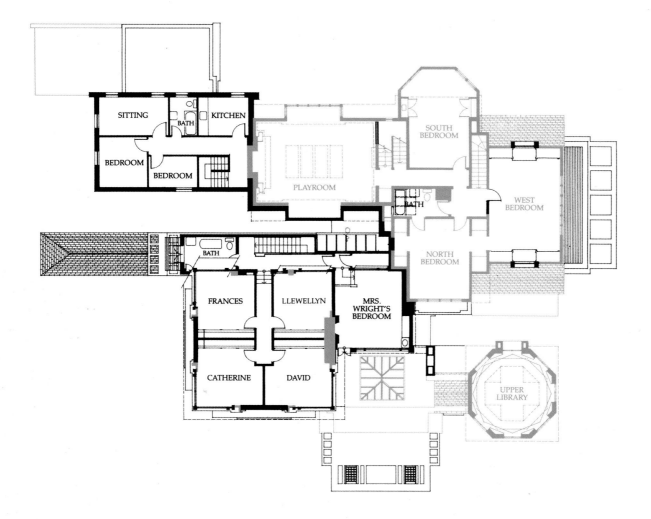

SITTING KITCHEN

BATH

BEDROOM

BEDROOM

PLAYROOM

SOUTH
BEDROOM

WEST
BEDROOM

BATH

NORTH
BEDROOM

BATH

FRANCES LLEWELLYN MRS.
WRIGHT'S
BEDROOM

CATHERINE DAVID

UPPER
LIBRARY

■ 1911 SECOND-FLOOR PLAN

On the second floor, the opening made by the drafting-room balcony was closed up, and the octagonal corners of the balcony drum were squared off to create bedroom space for the four younger children, who still lived at home. A bedroom for Catherine Wright was added above Wright's former office. Over the garage a separate apartment was built as a rental unit.

The firewall necessitated closing up the master-bedroom window in the closet, the Home bathroom window, the Home kitchen doors and windows and the north window bay of the playroom.

The firewall turned out to be a gold mine of information about the history of the building because it concealed data that provided clues about construction prior to 1911. Behind the firewall's double layer of bricks stood the 1898 plaster wall of the passageway between the Home and the Studio. The 1898 plaster showed the exact color of paint present in 1909, and the trim sample gave a size and a stain color. Beneath the 1898 plaster was red rosin paper, which was probably used as a barrier against the creosote stain on the shingles directly underneath. The shingles dated from 1898, when that surface was the exterior of the Home. The shingles' medium-brown creosote stain was probably the original color of the Home's exterior and the same one to which the exterior was restored, 1974. Photograph: Frank Lloyd Wright Preservation Trust.

One of the earliest events of the restoration took place in 1974 when, using historic plans, a volunteer crew plotted where the doorway had been located between the Home and the Studio. They then made the first opening between the two buildings in sixty-three years. The group styled themselves the "hole-in-the-wall gang" and posed by their hole in the brick firewall, where they found evidence of the original opening, walled up in 1911. Photograph: Frank Lloyd Wright Preservation Trust.

Catherine Wright and her children occupied the Studio part of the complex until 1918, when she and Llewellyn (by then, the only child left at home) moved into an apartment on Oak Park Avenue for a year and then to an apartment on Division Street in Chicago.

Both the Home and the Studio were rented until 1925, when Wright sold the property. He needed money to rebuild Taliesin, much of which had been destroyed in a disastrous fire that year. To ready the property for sale, Wright once again made modifications to the Home and Studio. Most notable was a bridge built to connect the apartment above the garage to the second floor above the former drafting room. The entire property was sold in mid-1925 for $33,500. For the next two decades, several owners and tenants occupied the building.

In 1946 Clyde and Charlotte Nooker bought the property, which had been divided into apartments during World War II. About 1956, the Nookers commissioned Wright to design a bath, lavatory, dressing area and kitchen to replace the 1911 kitchen and dining room. They planned to restore the building, and in July 1965, they opened parts of the building to visitors.

At that time, the complex was divided into six apartments:

THE RESTORED HOME AND STUDIO

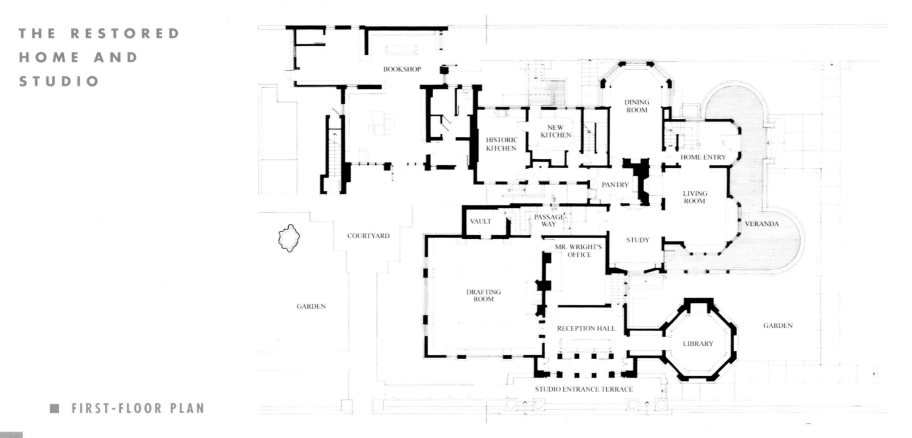

BOOKSHOP

DINING ROOM

NEW KITCHEN

HISTORIC KITCHEN

HOME ENTRY

PANTRY

LIVING ROOM

VAULT

PASSAGE-WAY

VERANDA

COURTYARD

STUDY

MR. WRIGHT'S OFFICE

GARDEN

DRAFTING ROOM

GARDEN

RECEPTION HALL

LIBRARY

STUDIO ENTRANCE TERRACE

■ FIRST-FLOOR PLAN

1. First-floor Home front apartment
2. First-floor Home rear apartment
3. Second-floor Home apartment
4. First-floor Studio apartment
5. Second-floor Studio apartment
6. Garage apartment

Although the scope of the restoration project was too large for the Nookers and many areas remained unfinished, they understood the importance of the building and cared for it as best they could. After Clyde Nooker's death in

1971, Charlotte Nooker tried to keep the building open to visitors, but with no more funds for restoration, she put it up for sale in 1972.

In 1974 the Frank Lloyd Wright Home and Studio Foundation purchased the building in partnership with the National Trust for Historic Preservation and embarked on its thirteen-year, close-to-$3 million, historically accurate restoration. ■

Drawings: Frank Lloyd Wright Preservation Trust.

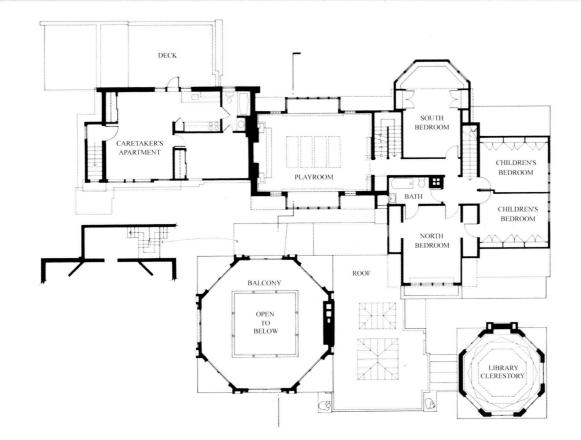

■ SECOND-FLOOR PLAN

Chapter 2

RALLYING TO SAVE A LANDMARK

Restoration committee members and guests at a dedication/fundraising event to commemorate the almost-completed dining room restoration, 1977. Photograph: Frank Lloyd Wright Preservation Trust.

When I look back on what made our project succeed, I realize the National Trust's deadline [to raise matching funds to purchase the property] was a large part of that success. . . . We had neither Madison Avenue public relations nor a finely honed professional fund-raising program. It was a people-to-people project run by volunteers who had little experience in this sort of thing, but who had a project all could believe in.

—Dawn Goshorn Schumann
First board president,
Frank Lloyd Wright Home and Studio Foundation

The Village of Oak Park has existed as an independent township since 1901. It shares the city of Chicago's western boundary and contains twenty-five buildings designed by Frank Lloyd Wright and the world's largest concentration of Prairie-style residences.

In the early 1970s, facing an eroding tax base, changing racial demographics and an alarming business decline, the Village embarked on an extensive planning process. One element of this process was the 1972 Hasbrouck-Sprague survey of local architecture. The survey revealed that the community had 328 buildings of historic significance, more per capita than any other community in the United States. It was fortunate to have also a responsive local government, supportive banks, a history of community involvement and a determination to make racial integration succeed. What the Village needed was a new industry. The Chicago Architecture Foundation had already begun offering architecture tours of Oak Park. All indicators pointed to cultural tourism as a potential answer, and in 1972 the Oak Park Landmarks Commission was formed. The following year, the Frank Lloyd Wright-Prairie School of Architecture Historic District was placed on the National Register of Historic Places.

Frank Lloyd Wright's own home and studio served as the cornerstone of historic architecture in Oak Park. Serendipitously, it was up for sale. The enthusiasm generated by efforts to purchase the building from its private owner and then restore it created a ripple effect. People from outside Oak Park bought houses in the area, and longtime residents gave considerable thought to what they already had. The restoration of the Home and Studio aided the development of a new attitude toward and an appreciation of architecture in the area. The interest encompassed Oak Park's grand collection of Prairie, Queen Anne, Arts and Crafts, Stick and vernacular-style homes. It did not take long for regional, national and international attention to focus on the Village and spawn a burgeoning tourism industry that still contributes significantly to the economic viability of the community. By 1976 Oak Park had revitalized itself enough to win the coveted All America City Award for the Oak Park Housing Center, Oak Park Mall and the Frank Lloyd Wright Home and Studio.

THE BIRTH OF THE FOUNDATION

In the summer of 1972, a group of preservation-minded Oak Parkers sought the assistance of the Oak Park Development Corporation (OPDC), a private development organization subsidized by the Village of Oak Park, to purchase Wright's home and studio, which had been owned by Mrs. Charlotte Nooker since the 1940s. After exerting great effort to return the building to its 1911 appearance and opening portions of it for tours, Mrs. Nooker hoped to sell her landmark property to a federal or local agency that would keep it open to the public. With the OPDC acting as an intermediary, she and the interested Oak Parkers accomplished their goal of preserving the property as a community asset.

It took almost two years of subtle negotiation with Mrs. Nooker to agree upon a purchase price of $168,000 in May 1974. With temporary financing arranged by Avenue Bank, the property was purchased by the Oak Park

Development Corporation and put into a land trust. No interest was required on the loan while the property was being held in trust.

The Frank Lloyd Wright Home and Studio Foundation was incorporated as a 501(c)3 public not-for-profit organization in June 1974. Its goals were to acquire the property, restore and preserve it, and operate it as a historic house museum.

Mrs. Charlotte Nooker, owner of Wright's home and studio in 1974, and Art Replogle, then president of the Oak Park Development Corporation, finalizing the sale agreement of the landmark property. Photograph: Oak Park Development Corporation.

The fledgling Foundation reached out to the National Trust for Historic Preservation, the country's most prestigious nonprofit organization devoted to saving and preserving structures of architectural and historic merit. At that time, federal funds were available to assist with acquisitions, enabling the National Trust to use Department of Interior funds to match those raised by the local community. The property would be owned by the National Trust, while the Foundation would be responsible for its restoration and operation under a long-term lease. This unique costewardship agreement was the first of its kind for the National Trust. A key factor in the National Trust's decision to agree to this arrangement was the strong support the cause received from citizen volunteers, Village government and the local financial and business community. If successful, the leaseback experiment would give the National Trust new operational flexibility, broadening its program without increasing the overhead costs of maintaining and operating buildings. For the Foundation, the arrangement would alleviate the pressure of having to meet a long-term mortgage obligation.

The Foundation was eventually required to raise almost $111,000 within six months to cover one-half of the purchase price, interest, fees and money for emergency repairs. An extraordinary effort to raise the money to satisfy the agreement ensued.

Under the terms of the costewardship agreement, the National Trust for Historic Preservation holds title to the property and leases it to the Frank Lloyd Wright Preservation Trust (then the Frank Lloyd Wright Home and Studio Foundation) for a token amount of $10 a year. The Frank Lloyd Wright Preservation Trust has full responsibility for and control over operation, restoration and preservation.

The two-story structure at the left is the studio-drafting room. The octagonal wing at the right is the library. Wright made this drawing in 1897. Changes since that time were made to the roof of the studio and to the entry (center).

Buy Wright home, studio

A heritage of greatness is secured

The Oak Park Development Corp. and a newly-formed Oak Park citizens' organization have purchased and will restore the Frank Lloyd Wright home and studio, 428 Forest Av. and 951 Chicago Av., Oak Park.

Wright designed the house in 1889 when only twenty-two years old and lived in it with his growing family for nearly twenty years. There and in the studio, added in 1895, he launched the renowned Prairie Style of architecture and drew plans for many other now-famous buildings, including Unity Temple in Oak Park and Robie House in Chicago.

The citizens' organization, a not-for-profit group formed especially for this purpose, is the Frank Lloyd Wright Home and Studio Foundation. All its officers are residents of Oak Park or River Forest. Arthur S. Replogle, president of the Oak Park Development Corp., will serve as foundation board chairman. The foundation's president is Dawn Follett Goshorn.

OTHER OFFICERS ARE Jerry D. Mackey, president of Avenue State Bank, Oak Park, first vice president; William Dring, architect, second vice president; Elsie Lundy Jacobsen, chairman of the Frank Lloyd Wright bus tour program, third vice president; John G. Thomson, legal counsel; Robert Wetzel, corporate secretary; Alice Wilcox, secretary; and Dennis G. Kenny, treasurer.

The home and studio were purchased from Mrs. Clyde Nooker for $168,000 with a temporary loan from Avenue State Bank. The other three Oak Park banks, Oak Park Trust and Savings Bank, First Bank of Oak Park, and Suburban Trust and Savings Bank, have indicated that they will participate in the permanent financing.

Richard Mehring of the Interior Department says such local financing of a landmark purchase is "very encouraging, and unusual in the sense that it's 100 percent funding. This is an awfully good show of faith by the financial community and the rest of the community."

Title to the property, which is on the southeast corner of Chicago and Forest Avs., is now held by Avenue Bank in trust for the Oak Park Development Corp. The corporation soon will assign its beneficial interest to the foundation.

WE ARE GRATEFUL to Mrs. Nooker for selling the property to us, and to both Mrs. Nooker and her late husband for their devoted stewardship extended over more than thirty years," Replogle says. "Aside from the cultural advantages of this acquisition, there have to be economic benefits to the community. For example

our chances of attracting new businesses such as restaurants and a motel are enhanced when we can say that the Wright house is open on a regular schedule for visitors."

The actual restoration and preservation of the home and studio will be undertaken by the newly-created foundation. According to Dring, the foundation intends to make a very careful restoration, down to the smallest detail, to recreate the home and studio as they were at the time Wright lived and worked here. This will be difficult, he says, because the architect enlarged and altered the building several times while living there. Other modifications, also designed by Wright, were made subsequently.

The eldest of Wright's seven children, Lloyd, who was born in the Forest Av. house in 1890, has agreed to assist the foundation in the restoration. Also an architect, Lloyd Wright, who lives in Los Angeles, will confer in Oak Park later this month with foundation officers and others who will assist in the restoration. The foundation intends to appoint an architectural advisory committee, composed of architects especially interested in Frank Lloyd Wright and his work, to advise the foundation on such matters as the priorities in the restoration work and the techniques to be used.

Mrs. Goshorn, says funds to repay the bank loans and for the restoration will be sought from individuals, foundations, state and federal agencies and the National Trust for Historic Preservation, a quasi-government organization in Washington D.C. The home and studio will continue to be open to the public, and, she says, visitors' admission fees will produce additional income for restoration and continuing maintenance of the property.

Mrs. Goshorn says the project greatly was aided by members of the Historical Society of Oak Park and River Forest; W. Brewer Grant, former director of the Oak Park-River Forest Community Chest; architectural historian Tom Slade and Mary Means of the National Trust for Historic Preservation, and to all other interested citizens "who did very helpful spadework and generated many ideas" leading to the formation of the foundation and the acquisition of the Wright property.

This view shows Wright's studio as it was when Wright worked there. The photo is from a German publication,"Ausgefuhrte Bauten", published in 1911.

OAK LEAVES

In 1976 the Frank Lloyd Wright Home and Studio was declared a National Historic Landmark. To qualify for this designation, a site needs to meet at least one of three criteria: have an association with an individual important to some aspect of American history; be the location of an event of national significance; or be of artistic merit in and of itself. As the dwelling of Frank Lloyd Wright, one of America's greatest architects, the birthplace of the Prairie style of architecture, and a building that reflects Wright's early experiments with architectural concepts, the Home and Studio is one of only a very few buildings to qualify for the designation on all three grounds. ▪

The acquisition and proposed restoration of the landmark property by the newly formed Foundation was hailed by the community press. Oak Leaves *news clipping, July 17, 1974. Photograph: Frank Lloyd Wright Preservation Trust.*

Every dollar counted in the six-month marathon to raise matching funds for half the purchase price of the Home and Studio. Photograph: Frank Lloyd Wright Preservation Trust.

Fundraising efforts to match the National Trust monies ranged from black-tie affairs to curbside lemonade stands. Less than three weeks before the deadline, the Foundation sponsored a tour of ten Wright-designed buildings in Oak Park and neighboring River Forest on May 24, 1975. At $25 a ticket, the event contributed almost $25,000. The "Ten by Wright Tour" was the first installment in what has grown into the eagerly anticipated yearly house walk called "Wright Plus," which draws an international audience to Oak Park.

On May 30, 1975, the Foundation presented a benefit at Chicago's Blackstone Theater. The audience was treated to a performance of Noel Coward's *In Two Keys* starring Anne Baxter (Wright's granddaughter), Hume Cronyn and Jessica Tandy.

The local press began a countdown to the deadline, reporting regularly on how much more money needed to be raised and how many days were left. Community groups rallied to the call. A check for $5 arrived with a note saying "Thank you for caring for America's heritage. Here's my dinner for tomorrow night." A Hungarian refugee who had once lived in Oak Park and who had been an architecture student in Hungary raised $200 from students at the university he was attending at that time. A thirteen-year-old boy walked into the Foundation's makeshift office with a flannel bag containing $101.35. He had been saving it for a new bicycle. When urged to keep the money, he announced Oak Park was his town too, then left the room—and the money—without giving his name.

Five days before the deadline, $3,500 was needed to reach the fundraising goal. A phone call arrived from the organizers of the local art fair. They had decided to make up the difference by donating $3,500 from that year's event.

You can take tours of a lot of other buildings where a tour guide recites a memorized script. Here, we give our volunteers a body of knowledge and expect them to choose the focus of what they want to say. When they look at the building, they want to share everything they know, which is why it can be hard for interpreters to give a forty-five-minute tour—they know too much. ■

—Jack Lesniak
Restoration committee and
interpreter committee chairman

FINANCIAL INDEPENDENCE

Tours were to be the new Foundation's main source of revenue, and on July 17, 1974, the Home and Studio formally reopened to the public. Admission cost $2. Volunteer docents were assigned to stand by and begin their tours when enough visitors had gathered. Soon the building was open twelve hours a week. Few dreamed there would come a time when it would be open 362 days a year and welcome more than 85,000 visitors annually. Frank Lloyd Wright's oldest son, Lloyd Wright, visited that summer. His memories of life in the building contributed greatly to the substance of the tours. He termed the docents "interpreters" because, as he said, it was their job to interpret the building. As research on the structure progressed and new information came to light, the tours evolved and a comprehensive training program for volunteers was developed. The Frank Lloyd Wright Preservation Trust's tour guides are still referred to as interpreters.

Setting for genius: The Wright way

The Oak Park studio-house where architect Frank Lloyd Wright lived and worked for two decades was opened to the public Saturday. For $2 admission, the setting for his genius was made public by the Wright nonprofit citizen group, at 951 Chicago, Oak Park. LEFT: Studio is on the left, next to the home. ABOVE RIGHT: Visitors sign in under leaded-glass skylight in studio hall. ABOVE LEFT: Playroom where the six Wright children were nurtured in childhood. Wright died in 1959. (Sun-Times Photos by Gene Pesek)

The first tour organized by the Frank Lloyd Wright Home and Studio Foundation received widespread coverage from the Oak Park and Chicago press. Chicago Sun-Times *news clipping, July 22, 1974. Photograph: Frank Lloyd Wright Preservation Trust.*

The 1911 garage was restored for adaptive use as a bookshop, keeping the area as close as possible to its original appearance. The bookshop doors are the original restored garage doors. Inside, the exposed brick walls and plumbing pipes on the ceiling were left uncovered. Photograph: Frank Lloyd Wright Preservation Trust.

In 1975 the Ginkgo Tree Bookshop, housed in the octagonal library of the Studio, opened its doors to provide another source of revenue and support the Foundation's educational mission. Staffed entirely by volunteers, this tiny shop soon outgrew its space and in 1979 moved to new quarters in the garage, which had been restored for adaptive use. Since then, the merchandising program has grown to include a catalog operation, an offsite distribution center and a second bookshop at the Frederick C. Robie House.

The Oak Park Tour Center was created by the Frank Lloyd Wright Home and Studio Foundation in 1975 to operate volunteer-led walking, bicycle and bus tours of the Historic District. The Foundation signed an agreement with the Village to operate the tour program and was compensated for its services and expenses. In 1979 a Visitors Center was opened at Lake Street and Forest Avenue, two blocks south of the Home and Studio. By the early 1990s

WRIGHT FAMILY INVOLVEMENT

When research for the restoration began, four of Frank Lloyd Wright's children were still alive: Lloyd Wright, David Wright, Catherine Wright Baxter and Robert Llewellyn Wright. They were extremely supportive of the Foundation, and their memories of life in the Oak Park Home were a major source of information about the site. Several of Wright's grandchildren—Eric Lloyd Wright (son of Lloyd Wright), Elizabeth Wright Ingraham (daughter of John Lloyd Wright), Anne Baxter (daughter of Catherine Wright Baxter) and Nora Natof (daughter of Frances Wright Natof)—also contributed to the Foundation's efforts with restoration advice and fundraising assistance. In addition, the family donated many valuable items pertaining to the family life in Oak Park to the Foundation's collections.

new local tour attractions had developed. Assuming responsibility for the now extraordinarily successful tourist industry in Oak Park went beyond the mission of the Frank Lloyd Wright Home and Studio Foundation. In 1992 the Oak Park Visitors Bureau was established to operate the Visitors Center and continue the function of monitoring and promoting tourism in the Village. ∎

In July 1974 Lloyd Wright returned to his childhood home in Oak Park to lend support to the new Foundation. That day, while walking from room to room, Lloyd was followed by a group of interpreters who recorded his every word for posterity. A respected architect and designer of the Hollywood Bowl in California, Lloyd served as an architectural consultant for the Foundation's early restoration efforts. After Lloyd's death in 1978, his son Eric took his place as architectural consultant.

Lloyd Wright and his son Eric Lloyd Wright at the Wright-Tobin family reunion in Oak Park, 1977. Photograph: Frank Lloyd Wright Preservation Trust.

Like his elder brother Lloyd, David Wright visited his former childhood home on many occasions. His fond recollections of the place served as an invaluable source of information during the restoration process. Prior to his death in 1997, David and his wife, Gladys, donated significant materials to the Foundation's collections, including many important pieces from his father's collection of Japanese prints and decorative objects as well as the photographs Wright took during his sojourn in Japan.

David Wright with restoration architect Ann Abernathy and director of research and restoration Donald Kalec. Photograph: Frank Lloyd Wright Preservation Trust.

The Wright and Tobin families at a family reunion held at the Home and Studio, 1977. Photograph: Frank Lloyd Wright Preservation Trust.

In October 1977 the Foundation invited Frank Lloyd Wright's family members and descendants of the Wright, Lloyd-Jones and Tobin clans to come to Oak Park for a family reunion at the Home and Studio. Among the great number in attendance were three of Wright's own children: David, Lloyd and Llewellyn (left to right, center row). Standing second and third from the left are Eric Lloyd Wright and Nora Natof. This Foundation-organized reunion was the first time many members of the extended Wright families had gathered together, and the event spawned subsequent annual reunions at Unity Chapel in Spring Green, Wisconsin.

Just east of the Home and Studio was a Gothic Revival house (c. 1866) that had been purchased by Frank Lloyd Wright's mother, Anna Lloyd Wright, at the same time Wright bought the corner lot on which he planned to build. In 1976 Lloyd Wright recommended relocating the museum offices from the Home to "Anna's House" next door. However, after striving to keep the Home and Studio financially stable, purchasing an additional building seemed out of the question. By 1982 escalating numbers of visitors had intensified demands upon the museum and a move was essential. "Anna's House" presented the ideal solution when it came on the market early that summer. The Foundation could not afford to buy it, however, and reached out to the Village of Oak Park for assistance. As part of its tourism initiative, the Village agreed to purchase the property for $98,000, remodel the house into two apartments and rent them out until the Foundation could raise the funds to purchase the property. In 1985 the Foundation was able to occupy the house, which has served as its administrative offices ever since. Much of the work to convert the house to office space was done by volunteers. ■

Anna Lloyd Wright's house, also on the property, was converted into office space for the Foundation. Photograph: Frank Lloyd Wright Preservation Trust.

A children's architecture workshop held in the Home playroom. Photograph: Frank Lloyd Wright Preservation Trust.

MISSION TO EDUCATE

A key aspect of the organization's mission has always been educating the public about Frank Lloyd Wright's work and the Prairie style of architecture. Wright's artistic and architectural principles, many of which are manifested in the Oak Park Home and Studio, form the educational focus. Besides serving as interpreters and working on the restoration itself, volunteers developed the Foundation's education program, which steadily evolved to comprise tours, lectures, children's programs, youth workshops and school outreach. The bookshop, with its extensive offerings of publications on Frank Lloyd Wright, was already critical to furthering the Foundation's educational objectives.

The Research Center was originally conceived as a repository to preserve the photographs, architectural drawings, written records and building fragments that document the Home and Studio restoration. Comprising over 20,000 visual resources and 2,775 objects, the restoration documentation collection remains the largest single collection within the Research Center's holdings.

From a desire to make the information gleaned from the restoration and preservation of the Home and Studio available to the public, the primary role of the Research Center evolved into one of public service. Materials relating to the life and work of Frank Lloyd Wright, the Prairie style and the Wright family were collected and a reference library amassed that specifically focuses on Wright and the Prairie style of architecture. Since 1987, the Research Center has been open to the general public free of charge and without appointment.

Librarians and trained professionals answer reference inquiries, provide scholars with access to rare materials, and assist students with research on topics related to Frank Lloyd Wright, the Prairie style, Chicago architecture and historic preservation. Videographers, authors and publishers frequently make use of historic images from the Research Center's growing visual resources collection. ■

Curatorial and collections staff prepare an exhibit in the Research Center. Photograph: Frank Lloyd Wright Preservation Trust.

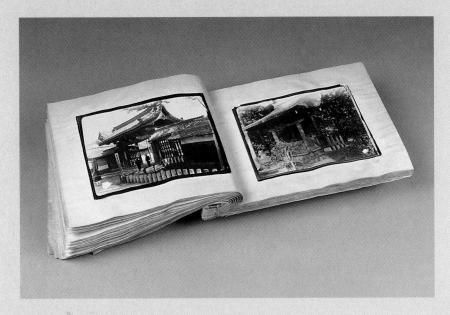

*Photograph album from the Wrights'
1905 trip to Japan. Photographs taken
by Frank Lloyd Wright. Gift of David
and Gladys Wright. Photograph: Frank
Lloyd Wright Preservation Trust.*

MUSEUM AND SPECIAL COLLECTIONS

In addition to the artifacts and furnishings on display in the Home and Studio interior, the Frank Lloyd Wright Preservation Trust continues to acquire historic materials and original objects to strengthen its museum and special collections. The basis of the museum collection is formed by the decorative arts collection, which includes over fifty original pieces of furniture and decorative objects and over one hundred art-glass windows, all designed by Wright. The Frank Lloyd Wright Preservation Trust's expanding museum and special collections demonstrate the influences on Wright during the early period of his career and provide a glimpse of his development as an architect and designer. Architectural fragments, drawings, rare books, historic periodicals and personal correspondence illuminate the social and architectural environment that surrounded Wright during the Prairie style period. Japanese prints, books and decorative objects owned by Wright attest to the architect's early passion for collecting Japanese materials.

The album of photographs taken by Wright during his first trip to Japan in 1905 (pictured here) is but one artifact from the substantial donation of materials that Wright family members have made to the Frank Lloyd Wright Preservation Trust over the years. Mr. and Mrs. David Wright's gifts to the special collections include such irreplaceable objects as family photographs; the family's china and silver; Wright's personal library from Oak Park; over 650 Japanese prints, textiles, and decorative objects; and architectural renderings and nature sketches drawn by Frank and Catherine Wright during the couple's honeymoon in 1889. Fine art, photographs, oriental carpets and numerous pieces of Wright-designed furniture original to the Home and Studio have been donated to the museum collections by Catherine Baxter, Robert Llewellyn Wright, Frances Lloyd Wright, Olgivanna Wright, Elizabeth Wright Ingraham, Anne Baxter, Eric Lloyd Wright, Thomas and Robert Wright, and Cameron and Jordan Wright. ■

A weekend work crew of volunteers taking a break during the restoration, 1981. Photograph: Frank Lloyd Wright Preservation Trust.

VOLUNTEER INVOLVEMENT

Hundreds of volunteers contributed countless hours to the restoration of the Home and Studio and the management of the young Foundation. They helped with demolition, stripped wood, painted the rooms, staffed the bookshop and the Visitors Center, did research, led tours, conducted workshops and raised much-needed funds. "It was a time I call Camelot," says the founding president, Dawn Goshorn Schumann, "when everyone focused on the same goal."

Chicago Avenue view of the building during restoration, 1984. Photograph: Frank Lloyd Wright Preservation Trust.

FRANK LLOYD WRIGHT HOME AND STUDIO

UNDERGOING HISTORIC RESTORATION TO 1909 DESIGN

Sometimes we undertake the battle for the wrong reasons, as when we wish to preserve something old just because it is old, or because we dislike what we know will replace it. Architectural quality and historical associations are not always found together. . . .

But there are happy hybrid occasions when history and art combine. Frank Lloyd Wright's Oak Park Home and Studio, besides being a work of art, albeit of domestic modesty, was the first-act setting for a drama of the inventive imagination that changed the course of architecture. No literate person can stand in those rooms without seeing ghosts, without hearing the arguments, the laughter, the ideas about how to live and build and make art, that are now part of everyone's history.

—Arthur Drexler, Director, Architecture and Design, Museum of Modern Art, New York
The Plan for Restoration and Adaptive Use of the Frank Lloyd Wright Home and Studio, 1978

Undertaking the restoration and conservation of an historically and architecturally significant structure is the most dramatic and public face of historic preservation. Before the process can begin, however, many complex questions about the philosophy and methodology behind the restoration need to be considered: What documentation about the building is available? What kinds of records need to be kept? Should all the original fabric be conserved? To what date should the building be restored? How will the building be adapted for its proposed use? How will it be furnished? How will the public be educated about the process? What funding sources are available? Which professionals will be best suited to perform the work?

In the case of Frank Lloyd Wright's Oak Park Home and Studio, the decisions were all the more complicated by the fact that Wright himself had made numerous changes to the structure over the course of many years. At no point had an "as-built" plan been drawn of the entire complex. John Lloyd Wright's drawing for the building's sale brochure in 1925 came close, but it did not contain exact measurements. Besides, many undocumented alterations to the building were made after the 1920s.

When the Foundation acquired the Home and Studio in 1974, three projects were undertaken immediately: emergency repairs to stabilize the building, physical documentation of the building to produce measured drawings documenting changes to the structure, and development of a comprehensive research program to shape the restoration as well as to help train volunteer interpreters.

RESTORATION PHILOSOPHY AND METHODOLOGY

To the uninformed visitor in 1974, the building gave no hint of the architectural innovation that had flourished there through the 1890s and the early 1900s. Nor did the building reveal the Wrights' rich family life and the

ways in which it was affected by the Home's architecture. The building was, in fact, as project architect Ann Abernathy put it, "like a barnacled old oyster, the clarity of the shell submerged in years of accretions." Wright's many changes and the later division of the building into rental units had diminished its ability to tell the story of Wright's original occupancy. Indeed, the Foundation's early tours asked visitors to imagine what magnificent spaces and vibrant lifestyle must have existed within those walls.

The goal of the restoration was to re-create the interior and exterior of the building as it appeared in 1909, the last year that Frank Lloyd Wright lived in the Home and used the Studio for his creative work. Restoration to this time period provides visitors with an authentic experience of Wright's evolving design attitudes during his years at the Oak Park Home and Studio. Educational and interpretive programs continue to support this goal.

This was a pioneer restoration of an early Frank Lloyd Wright building, and the restoration architects had few precedents to follow in terms of historic preservation or building restoration. Since then, the world of historic preservation has advanced so greatly that today the same architects might make different decisions about certain aspects, benefiting from the latest developments in the field. The Foundation's restoration of the Home and Studio was considered to be a model project. In February 1987, the American Institute of Architects bestowed a National Honor Award on the Foundation in recognition of the thirteen-year restoration.

While restoration projects generally have a single architect in charge, the Foundation instead established a volunteer restoration committee responsible for planning and executing restoration decisions. This group included restoration architects, engineers, landscape architects, art and architectural historians, and Foundation as well as community volunteers. Although a core team of architects led the effort, including preparing *The Plan for Restoration and*

Adaptive Use of the Frank Lloyd Wright Home and Studio (1978), all decisions were made through careful consensus building. Sometimes this required months of research or hiring special consultants to assist in testing materials and methods. Once every detail of the restoration design was established, the committee would hire and supervise contractors who completed the projects. So great were the advantages of bringing a variety of backgrounds to bear on restoration decisions that this procedure, along with an in-house architectural staff, is being repeated with the Frank Lloyd Wright Preservation Trust's current restoration of Wright's 1910 Frederick C. Robie House.

A number of philosophical principles guided the Home and Studio's restoration. Although achieving the restoration objectives required serious physical intervention to the existing building, conservation (minimal intervention to keep an artifact in its found state) and preservation (protection of an artifact with no intervention) were the priorities whenever practical. The restoration architects sought to conserve as much original building fabric as possible, thereby minimally affecting the building. At times, the mandate to preserve original material complicated and prolonged the process. Questions of restoration, conservation, preservation and reconstruction were constantly addressed as the committee had to make decisions, particularly involving the removal of Wright's remodelings of 1911 and 1956, in order to conform to the 1909 restoration target date.

Another central tenet was the accuracy of reproduction materials. From paint colors and plaster finishes to flooring materials and art glass, the committee took great care to reproduce authentically items that had been lost. This required attention to the minutest detail. For example, the restoration architects removed lacquer from new brass plates so that they would age naturally. In the interest of authenticity, they even re-created old processes like the mixing and laying of the floors made of magnesite, a turn-of-the-century building material.

In order to withstand the impact of thousands of visitors and meet current building codes for Assembly Occupancy, several structural adaptations were needed. For instance, to accommodate the heavier loading, the Studio's new foundation was built with 16-inch concrete walls to replace the lightweight, disintegrating 8-inch brick walls and piers. Steel I-beams reinforced wood framing in the Studio balcony, the living room ceiling and other areas. The flat, original tin roofs were replaced with gray lead-coated copper, and the tarred felt roofing was replaced with more durable single-ply membranes. To protect the museum collections, a state-of-the-art computer-controlled climate control system was installed. Great care was taken to ensure that all the adaptations were visually unobtrusive.

Despite extensive investigative probes before the contractors started restoration in a specific area, it was expected that workers would uncover more information or objects that they might not recognize as significant and either intentionally or unintentionally destroy them. For that reason, and to record every stage of work done, a staff architect was always on site to oversee the work.

While the restoration architects avoided any exploratory probes into surfaces they knew would be retained intact, as the time approached to begin that particular restoration project, they had a specific plan of what was to be removed. The plan included a list of questions about what features could be discovered by examination of the structure once demolition began, so all knew what to look for as the removal process proceeded.

Documentation through photographs, drawings and field notes was an important component of the restoration process, particularly since original

Wright-designed material was being removed and few other construction drawings of the building existed. Documentation served four purposes: to record existing conditions, record work performed, provide useful preventive maintenance information, and satisfy the Foundation's educational goal of making information about the restoration available to the public. The Foundation's Research Center was established in 1977 as a repository for this information. It has since added extensive collections focused on Frank Lloyd Wright and the Prairie style of architecture.

The re-creation of Wright's living and working environments was achieved through the implementation of an acquisitions plan. (See sidebar, "Furnishing the Home and Studio.")

The progress of the restoration always depended on the availability of funding. Larger projects were taken on as fundraising goals were achieved; smaller projects were sometimes tackled by volunteers. The restoration plan included sixteen phases that ranged from building stabilization and exterior restoration to interior restoration and furnishing. Most of the research on the complex was conducted between 1974 and 1981, before actual restoration work started. However, the dining room was restored as early as 1977 so as to act as a model for the restoration quality the Foundation could achieve.

Reconstruction of the Studio (1982–84) preceded the restoration of the Home mainly because the Studio needed such extensive structural work. The Home's restoration was performed primarily between 1985 and 1987. Long before it began in earnest, however, while early emergency repairs were being carried out, volunteers had painted the rooms to make them presentable for visitors. All these rooms were repainted in their historic colors after the structural work was completed. Interior restoration remains an ongoing process as the museum collections grow and installations are revis-

ited to evoke family and work life in the Home and Studio between 1904 and 1909 as authentically as possible.

Through the entire restoration, the site remained open for tours even though not all areas were always accessible. Visitors, volunteers and staff found the planning and monthly progress fascinating, and the Foundation fulfilled its key objectives of maintaining public accessibility and education.

DETERMINING THE RESTORATION TARGET DATE

One of the major questions the restoration committee faced was determining the appropriate date to which to restore the building. In 1974 the building was basically in its condition of 1911, when Wright had converted it into a duplex. He had remodeled it again in 1956 for the Nookers, the owners at the time, and they had subdivided as well as partially restored it to the 1911 period. The discussion about the restoration target date took into account the three criteria that qualified the Home and Studio to be a National Historic Landmark: (1) Frank Lloyd Wright, one of America's greatest architects, lived here; (2) the uniquely American Prairie style of architecture evolved here; and (3) the building itself illustrated many of the Master's architectural concepts.

Four options for a target date were considered. The first was to preserve the building essentially as it was, since Frank Lloyd Wright had directed much of the remodeling. This scheme was rejected because the committee felt the real significance of the structure came from the earlier use of the complex, when it housed Wright's family and his architectural practice. The later alterations obscured much of this purpose. There was no trace of the family life that had been so bound up in the Home's design. The Studio, where the Prairie style of architecture was developed, was gone. Wright's adaptation of his studio to a living space for his family was called "make-do" by Lloyd Wright, who did not consider it worthy of restoration. To preserve the building as it was would have meant letting it remain a complex of apartments. Additionally, there was a significant amount of work needed just to stabilize the building. Structural areas needed strengthening, rotting wood framing had to be replaced, and inadequate foundations needed to be rebuilt. All these projects would have involved altering the property's existing condition. Moreover, since the entire Studio area would have required extensive structural work with drastic intervention anyway, the restoration committee considered restoring its appearance to the time when it housed Wright's architectural practice.

The second possibility was to preserve the "best elements" ranging from 1889 to 1957, capturing the "spirit of Wright." Defining "best" was immediately recognized as a problem. The committee concluded that this option would result in a structure that never really existed in history. The relationship of spaces to one another, so important to Wright, would have been confusing. Components from one era, such as the low, horizontal Roman brick fireplace (1911), placed in a space from another era, namely the high two-story drafting room (1898), would have been out of context. National preservation policies rejected such anachronisms.

The third scheme was rigid adherence to a given restoration date, such as 1909, the last year Frank Lloyd Wright lived and worked in the building. Since no exceptions would be permitted, this option was rejected, as it severely limited the possibility of adaptive use. The restoration committee would have had to raze usable areas such as the attached garage and its second-story apartment at the rear of the property. From the beginning, the committee realized that in order to serve the educational and interpretive goals of the Foundation, it would be necessary to use any available space creatively and efficiently—as long as doing so did not obscure the major spaces.

The final possibility was to focus on a specific date to which to restore the building, but to allow for certain reasonable exceptions. Lesser elements, such as the garage and its apartment, could be utilized to support the Foundation's functions. The committee planned this adaptive use in such a way as to leave these post-1909 additions intact, thereby allowing the option of their future restoration. This plan for adherence to a primary date with limited latitude for adaptive use became the committee's recommended option.

The committee took the position that 1909, the last year Wright lived in the Home and worked in the Studio, was the most appropriate date to which to restore the property. The selection of this date necessitated actions that were quite difficult and sometimes controversial. At the center of the debate were three major 1911 elements slated for removal: a cantilevered overhang at the Studio entrance, a Roman brick fireplace in the drafting room and a private walled garden adjacent to Wright's Studio office. Along with other noteworthy features from Wright's 1911 remodeling, such as the Home's 1911 automobile entrance, these had to be removed in order to keep the clarity sought by adherence to the target date. By taking out some of the later work, the committee was able to create the unified aesthetic experience that existed in 1909 and to showcase the "total environment" for which Wright strove. When conflicting or insufficient evidence made certain decisions too arbitrary (as with the fireplace in the octagonal library), existing conditions were preserved as recommended by current preservation ethics.

The proposed target date for the Home and Studio's restoration was discussed and approved by a panel of Wright experts and restoration architects at a 1977 conference hosted by the Frank Lloyd Wright Home and Studio Foundation.

RESEARCH METHODS

The restoration committee undertook a comprehensive research program before beginning work on the Home and Studio. More than 180 historic interior and exterior photographs, including some taken by Wright, were acquired from various archives and individuals. They provided a wealth of information about the building throughout its history and were some of the most valuable resources consulted by the committee. The only drawback was that many of the photographs were not dated, and they had to be used in conjunction with other data in order to establish a correct chronology of the property. These photographs are in the Frank Lloyd Wright Preservation Trust's Research Center and are consulted regularly by scholars, students and videographers.

A limited number of Wright drawings of the buildings existed in the archives of the Frank Lloyd Wright Foundation at Taliesin West in Scottsdale, Arizona, and at the Avery Architecture and Fine Arts Library, Columbia University, New York City. The committee obtained and studied copies that included ten drawings of the Home from 1889 and a few sketches of the Studio. The restoration architects also consulted the 1925 sale brochure and the as-built sketches from which it was prepared. These later drawings showed the building essentially in the configuration that resulted from Wright's 1911 remodeling.

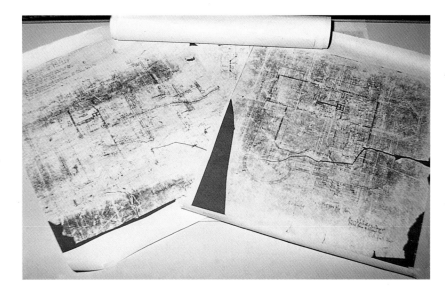

Archival architectural drawings were another source of information. Photograph: Donald Kalec. Frank Lloyd Wright Preservation Trust.

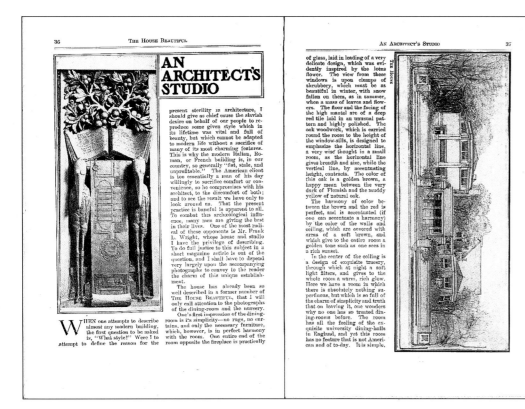

Published materials from Wright's time contained details about the building's interior not found anywhere else. Photograph: Frank Lloyd Wright Preservation Trust.

The restoration committee also collected contemporary published materials on the Home and Studio. Periodical articles about the property provided detailed information—most notably, Alfred H. Granger's description of Wright's home in *House Beautiful* of February 15, 1897, and his article titled "An Architect's Studio," in a December 1899 issue of the same magazine.

Legal documents, such as deeds, liens and building permits not only revealed details about the state of the property but also led the committee to former owners and occupants who provided more information about the building.

. . . Father was very fond of gathering family and friends into the studio for an oyster roast. Also, I recall that my two aunts, his sisters, were married in the studio, and we all participated in these affairs.

One Christmas, I recall father had been very busy on some creative plans, was reminded by Mother that he had done nothing about our Christmas holiday gifts, whereupon he gathered us all together and marched us down Lake Street to a local hardware store where we each picked out a sled for our Merry Christmas. . . .

We were always up early on Christmas morning and had to wait until Father put on his robe and made his way down the long corridor since he was the one who lit all the candles on the tree before we were allowed to rush down the hall. I am sure he handed out the presents to us with real ceremony. ■

—Catherine Baxter
Excerpt from a 1976 letter to Donald Kalec,
Research Center director

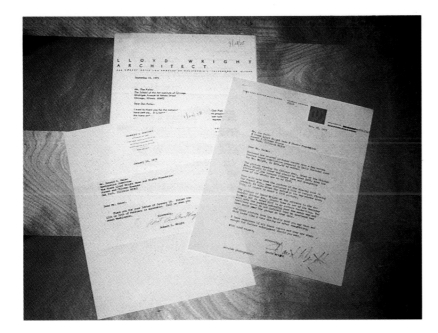

Members of the Wright family offered their memories of life in their childhood home. Photograph: Donald Kalec. Frank Lloyd Wright Preservation Trust.

Donald Kalec, who became the Foundation's director of research and restoration, interviewing Lloyd Wright and his son, Eric Lloyd Wright, 1976. Photograph: Tom Heinz. Frank Lloyd Wright Preservation Trust.

Correspondence from Wright's relatives augmented the prerestoration research with insights into the history of the property and the Wright family. It also enriched the development of interpretive material for use in public tours.

Interviews with Catherine and Frank Lloyd Wright's children (Lloyd, Catherine, David and Llewellyn) living at that time gave insights into the building and family life and provided lively, compelling material that was used in the interpretation of the property for the public. Occasionally the children's memories of the building and the physical evidence conflicted. Negotiating these matters became an intriguing challenge for the restoration committee. Lloyd Wright, a respected architect, initially took the lead in representing the family. The Foundation's early interpretive tours were largely based on Lloyd's reminiscences about life in the Home and Studio. After his death in 1978, his brother David became the family spokesperson and a key restoration consultant.

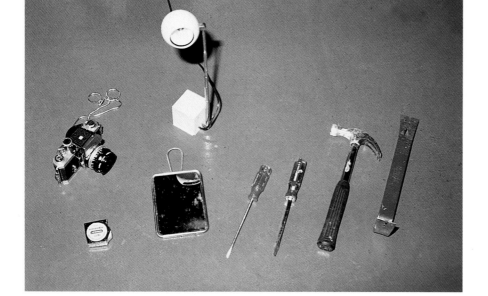

Simple implements such as mirrors, flashlights and cameras were used to probe the building for clues to its past. Photograph: Donald Kalec. Frank Lloyd Wright Preservation Trust.

Lloyd Wright was an inspiring tower of strength, a lumbering giant with a heart of gold. [As with] his father, money was not a consideration. Lloyd suggested that Oak Park construct an overpass on Chicago Avenue and a parking lot for visitors under the Holmes School playground [across the street from the Home and Studio]—all at a time when his father's reputation was decidedly not positive! He was determined that our plans should be sound and authentic and, most of all, [they] had to be in the spirit of Wright. Lloyd crackled with indignation at the lack of respect [some showed] his father's work, and urged us to preserve the Wright legacy. ■

—Lyman Shepard
Founding board member

Every old building offers clues to its past if one knows where and what to seek. The most significant source of information, therefore, was the building itself. Using simple tools like those shown, the restoration architects probed the walls, floors and ceilings through small holes bored in patchable areas, searching for clues that would shed light on the structure's past.

When Frank Lloyd Wright experimented with design and made changes to his building, he almost never removed anything, but rather built directly on top of what existed. As a result, the restoration architects' sleuthing was often richly rewarded. Seemingly insignificant evidence such as the location of a nail hole, size of a stud, cuts in studs, and sheathing sizes provided important clues as to the dates of certain changes. Areas of archaeological probes were photographed, and the data were used to confirm suspected alterations to the building. As assumptions proved correct, the architects were emboldened to remove larger areas of plaster and trim in areas that were slated for demolition in order to get closer to the 1909 configuration. Evidence from such probes was pieced together with data from historic photographs, drawings, paint analyses and oral histories.

John G. Thorpe, architect and chairman of the restoration committee, performing an above-grade archaeological probe. Photograph: Donald Kalec. Frank Lloyd Wright Preservation Trust.

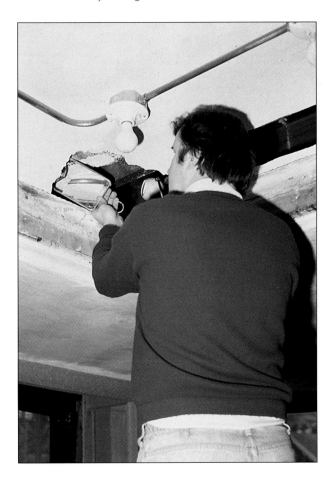

Undated photograph (probably c. 1911) showing construction of the garden wall. The Home roof has two dormers on the north side. Research into the date when the dormer was built (c. 1911) helped determine that the wall came after 1909. Photocopy in the collection of the Frank Lloyd Wright Preservation Trust.

The data only made complete sense when combined. For instance, an undated photograph showed the high brick wall of the enclosed studio garden under construction. In the background we could see a dormer window in the Home roof. An early interview with Lloyd Wright suggested that the dormers came in or after 1911, and paint analysis of the plaster inside the dormer confirmed this. We could therefore assume that the wall was built after 1909. Now we had another key to dating any elements that it was built on top of, a key to use in the next deductive sequence. ■

Ann Abernathy, project architect
"Outline: Restoration Alternatives, Goals and Procedures," 1985

And it is quite impossible to consider the building one thing and its furnishings another, its setting and environment still another. In the spirit in which these buildings are conceived, these are all one thing, to be foreseen and provided for in the nature of the structure.

—Frank Lloyd Wright
Studies and Executed Buildings of Frank Lloyd Wright, 1910

Frank Lloyd Wright firmly believed that furnishings were not secondary elements. He strove to create a holistic aesthetic environment that included landscape, architecture, furniture and decorative arts. Along with the architectural restoration, the restoration committee developed a plan for furnishing the Home and Studio museum in the most authentic manner possible, evoking approximately the last five years that the entire Wright family lived in the Home and Frank Lloyd Wright worked in his studio—c. 1904 through 1909.

Using all the historic photographs of the Home and Studio, a furniture and decorative arts survey was completed. Each object in each picture was assigned a discrete number, and research was conducted by committee members in consultation with decorative arts specialists to identify objects and ascertain their provenance.

The committee drew up an acquisitions plan that laid down an overarching philosophy for acquisition of interior furnishings and set priorities for use of the Foundation's limited funds. In accordance with the goal to furnish the Home and Studio as authentically as possible, original objects used by the Wright family in the 1904–09 Home and Studio, especially those pieces of furniture and decorative objects designed by Frank Lloyd Wright, were designated as highest priority. When it was not possible to acquire original objects that the Wrights owned while they were in residence, period furnishings designed by Wright and other objects that matched those shown in historic photographs were selected. Also, reproductions were created by exactly measuring originals or by carefully scaling historic photographs that showed original furniture. Many pieces of furniture and decorative arts were returned to the Home and Studio through the auspices of Wright's relatives. The Wright and Tobin families donated a great number of these items, while others were made available for purchase. ■

Paint analyst Robert Furhoff analyzed and assigned dates to the many layers of paint in the Home and Studio. Photograph: Frank Lloyd Wright Preservation Trust.

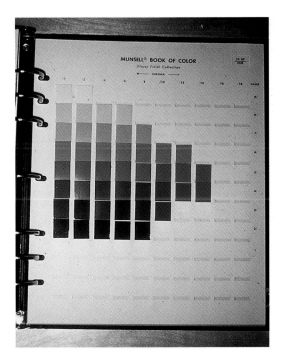

Paint colors in specific rooms were categorized in a chart according to the Munsell Color System, a standard color analysis technique. Photograph: Frank Lloyd Wright Preservation Trust.

Fragments of plaster, fabric and trim found during probes as well as at the time of construction. Photograph: Frank Lloyd Wright Preservation Trust.

Five separate paint analyses were conducted to determine the colors of the early building and double-check previous findings in specific rooms. The first analysis was conducted by the National Trust for Historic Preservation, and the other four were performed by a private paint consultant. In sections of the building that were put in place in 1911, the paint analysts determined the 1911 layer of paint and were then able to establish the coat below the 1911 layer as the 1909 layer. Wright was absent from Oak Park between 1909 and 1911, and it is unlikely the building was painted between those dates. Each coat of paint was matched to color categories in the Munsell Color System. The result was a complete chronology of the original paint layer and numerous repaintings of the Home and Studio. In some places,

behind trim or built-ins, the restoration architects found exposed 1909 colors, which ensured even greater accuracy.

Artifacts from the above-grade archaeology as well as those found during construction were cataloged and preserved in the Research Center. They ranged from large beams and plumbing fixtures to scraps of fabric. Also discovered were articles of clothing, utensils, letters, canceled checks and toys—all of which helped uncover a small piece of the past. Having a restoration architect always on site ensured that such treasures would be preserved. Paint and plaster samples from every wall and ceiling were saved for future analysis and research, especially since the technology of paint analysis advances every year.

RESTORATION DRAWINGS

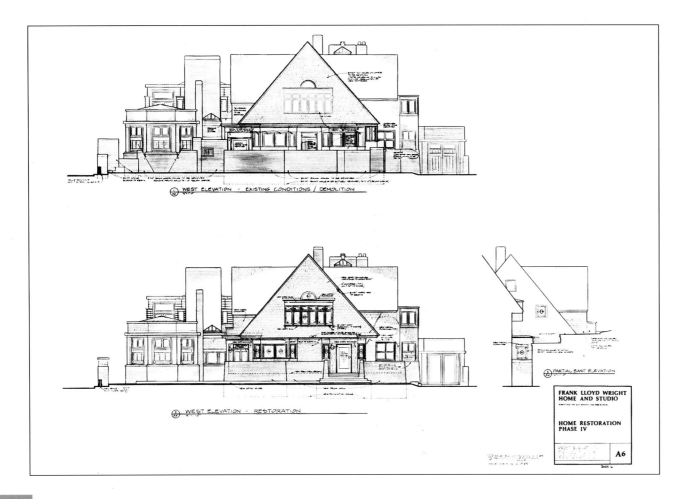

WEST ELEVATION · EXISTING CONDITIONS / DEMOLITION

WEST ELEVATION · RESTORATION

PARTIAL EAST ELEVATION

FRANK LLOYD WRIGHT
HOME AND STUDIO

HOME RESTORATION
PHASE IV

A6

Drawings such as this west elevation of the Home were developed to document existing conditions as well as to show the extent of restoration to be performed, 1985. Drawing: Frank Lloyd Wright Preservation Trust.

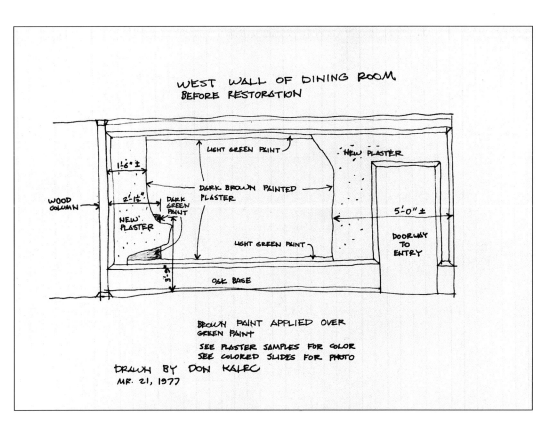

By the time the restoration began in earnest, the Foundation had amassed more than 250 as-built drawings of the property, most of which had been produced by the restoration committee or the restoration architects. The collection, which continued to grow as the restoration progressed, was divided into several categories.

Physical documentation or measured drawings were commissioned by the Foundation and accurately described the building when it was acquired. They also served as base drawings for restoration projects. As the projects were completed, these drawings were reproduced and revised to reflect the finished work.

Another category consisted of research drawings. As historical information was obtained, it was translated to a series of plan and elevation drawings reflecting specific time periods. Drawings in this category were modified as new research became available.

Design drawings were developed to illustrate the scope of the restoration and communicate it to the general public. They were published in *The Plan for Restoration and Adaptive Use of the Frank Lloyd Wright Home and Studio* (1978) and differentiated between the existing conditions and the proposed changes.

Finally, specific construction working drawings or blueprints were executed for each restoration project by the restoration architects. These served as the contract documents given to contractors hired to perform work.

At the 1977 conference to review the plan for restoration, (from left) Bruce Goff, Theodore Sande (observer, NTHP), H. Allen Brooks, Lloyd Wright and Eric Lloyd Wright. Photograph: Frank Lloyd Wright Preservation Trust.

RESTORATION MASTER PLAN

By 1977 the restoration committee had completed a master plan for the restoration and adaptive use of the Home and Studio. On October 31, 1977, the Foundation presented a draft to a ten-member panel. Participating in the discussion were Bruce Goff and John Howe, architects and associates of Frank Lloyd Wright; Arthur Drexler, director of architecture and design, the Museum of Modern Art, New York; H. Allen Brooks, professor of art, University of Toronto, and author of *The Prairie School* and numerous scholarly articles about Frank Lloyd Wright; Richard Frank FAIA, and representative of the National Trust for Historic Preservation; Frederick Gutheim, Ph.D., director, Department of Urban Planning, George Washington University, and editor of *Frank Lloyd Wright on Architecture,* an anthology of Wright's writings; Wilbert

Hasbrouck FAIA, editor and publisher of the *Prairie School Review;* Paul Sprague, Ph.D., visiting associate professor, University of Wisconsin, a preservation consultant and author of scholarly articles on Wright and Louis Sullivan; Lloyd Wright, architect, landscape architect and oldest son of Frank Lloyd Wright; and Eric Lloyd Wright, architect and Lloyd's son.

It was at this conference that, after spirited debate, the Foundation's decision to restore the building to its 1909 condition was ratified. Although the majority of the panelists agreed with this approach, there was considerable discussion about the exact manner in which to best implement this decision. The conference gave the restoration committee invaluable input and also served to raise public awareness of the project.

The Plan for Restoration and Adaptive Use of the Frank Lloyd Wright Home and Studio, *now out of print, was first published in 1978. Photograph: Frank Lloyd Wright Preservation Trust.*

Once the plan was finalized, it was published by the University of Chicago Press. *The Plan for Restoration and Adaptive Use of the Frank Lloyd Wright Home and Studio* documented the history of the site through text and drawings, explained the rationale for the restoration target date of 1909, presented the scope of restoration work, and outlined the Foundation's goals for adaptive use of the property and educational initiatives.

The master plan was systematically implemented over the next ten years, with only a few changes made when new information was uncovered during construction.

The Home's west façade, framed by the natural "tangle-wood" that filled the lot, c. 1889–90. Photograph: Frank Lloyd Wright Preservation Trust.

I turned to Mr. Sullivan with a new idea. "Mr. Sullivan, if you want me to work for you as long as five years, couldn't you lend me enough money to build a little house, and let me pay you back so much each month—taken out of my pay envelope?"

Mr. Sullivan—it seemed—had a good deal of money of his own at the time. He took me to his lawyer, Felsenthal. The contract was duly signed, and then the Master went with me—"the pencil in his hand"—to Oak Park to see the lot I knew I wanted. It was Mr. Austin's gardener's, the plain lot, the lovely old tanglewood. The lot was on Forest and Chicago Avenues. The Master approved the lot and bought it. There was $3,500 left over to build a small home on that ground planted by the old Scottish landscape-gardener.

"Now look out, Wright!" said Mr. Sullivan, "I know your tastes . . . no extras."

I agreed. "No, none."

But there was $1,200 more to be paid toward the end. I kept this in the dark, paid it in due course out of what remained of my salary.

—Frank Lloyd Wright
An Autobiography, 1943

Frank Lloyd Wright wrote in the introduction to his 1910 *Ausgeführte Bauten und Entwürfe von Frank Lloyd Wright:* "In America each man has a peculiar, inalienable right to live in his own house in his own way. He is a pioneer in every right sense of the word. His home environment may face forward, may portray his character tastes, and ideas, if he has any, and every man here has some somewhere about him."

Wright's first home portrays the man and the architect. It is suffused with his thoughts and actions, his family and architectural life, his core being. The spaces and objects he surrounded himself with reflect who he was, how he thought and felt. Throughout his twenty-year residency, Wright used his home as a laboratory in which to experiment with his evolving creative concepts. This abode provides a unique window through which to examine the life and philosophy of the young architect.

The restoration of the Home to the way it appeared in 1909 followed three main stages. In 1976, following preliminary research on the building, stabilization of the building was carried out: emergency repairs on the roof, exterior walls, chimneys and conservation of some of the art-glass windows. Next, in 1977, the Foundation restored the dining room as its first large-scale restoration project, to serve as a showcase and provide fundraising opportunities. Nearly a decade later, in 1985–86, the remaining interior and exterior restoration was completed with a generous grant from the Steelcase Corporation.

EARLY HOME RESTORATION PROJECTS

The restoration of the Home took place in several phases. Before the large-scale restoration projects of 1982–86 (the reconstruction of the Studio and major restoration of the Home), a number of projects were completed in the Home by volunteers under the guidance of the restoration architects:

- Removal of the front porch's roof and columns
- Restoration of the lunette window on the west façade
- Partial restoration of the playroom—ceiling grille, mural, wood surfaces, paint colors, floor, reinstallation of a hanging grand piano
- Restoration of the Home's woodwork to its original color and finish (including floors)
- Restoration of Catherine's dayroom—floor, art glass, fabric on walls, stencil, cabinet work
- Restoration of most of the Home's art glass
- Restoration of historic lighting in the living room, including restoration of decorative plaster corner plaques
- Restoration of the living room inglenook, including mirror and cushions
- Restoration of the dining room ■

West façade of the Home in 1974, when the Foundation acquired the property. Photograph: Donald Kalec. Frank Lloyd Wright Preservation Trust.

■ EXISTING CONDITIONS

When the Frank Lloyd Wright Home and Studio Foundation acquired the property in 1974, the Home retained many of the changes Wright had made to it in 1911 before leaving Oak Park, along with other changes to the building since 1911. On the front of the Home, Wright had made the following alterations:

- Added a large porch below the band of casement windows.
- Closed off a small lunette window centered above the casements.
- Repositioned the door between the two bays so that it no longer functioned as the main entrance, but just as a way to go out onto the front veranda. The main entrance was moved to the south side of the house.
- Removed the southern semicircular veranda to accommodate an automobile entrance on the south.
- Roofed over the front veranda and added four wood and brick piers along with a projecting trellis.

After the purchase of the land, Frank Lloyd Wright had $3,500 left from Sullivan's loan plus $1,200 of his own funds to put toward building his home. Construction and structure were conventional: rubble-stone foundation walls, a brick veneer base, solid brick veranda walls with limestone caps, balloon wood framing, 1 X 12-inch sheathing boards covered with building paper, wood shingles and a cedar-shingled roof laid over spaced sheathing boards. All floors were oak except for a maple kitchen floor and a basswood floor in the master bedroom. The terraces were floored with spaced 1 X 3-inch pine boards. Exterior wood trim was painted a light green, the

- Built a low decorative concrete wall along Forest Avenue and a high brick wall topped with decorative concrete units along Chicago Avenue.

Exterior restoration of the Home involved the reconstruction of numerous 1909 elements and the removal of various 1911 features in order to re-create the historically accurate façade.

The interior of the Home had been divided into three rooming apartments in the 1950s and 1960s. The Nookers, who occupied the building until they sold it to the Foundation, had rented out the Home's kitchen and maid's room as one apartment, and the living room and study as a second apartment. Both these areas had had bathrooms added to them. The dining room, which formed part of the rear apartment, was opened for short tours by the Nookers. The upstairs had been converted into a third apartment containing the playroom (as living room), master bedroom (as kitchen), bath, and south and west bedrooms. The Nookers included the second floor in their tours. By 1974, the room relationships and flow of open space were seriously interrupted, and certain architectural features that existed from 1889 to 1909 were obscured.

cedar shingles were left to weather, and the Chicago common-brick base was a buff color. Later, when a dark creosote stain was applied to the shingles and the brick (for weather protection), the green trim was darkened to a deep olive color.

In general, the Home had been very well constructed in 1889, and so was in fairly good shape. It required two major structural projects: (1) the entire front veranda was rebuilt because of inadequate foundations, and (2) the rubble-stone basement walls (on the west and south sides) were waterproofed and insulated so that the basement could be used for storage. A footing drain was also added. ■

■ HOME EXTERIOR

Almost immediately after the Foundation acquired the Home and Studio in 1974, emergency repairs were carried out to stabilize the building. The chimneys were lined to prevent water penetration and a new roof was installed. In the photograph of early repairs, layers of asphalt shingles are being torn off down to the original wood sheathing. New cedar shingles were then put in place and allowed to weather before the appropriate historical stain was applied.

The photograph on the right, dated c.1925, shows the original 1889 veranda on the west façade now covered with a flat roof and wooden trellis overhang supported by columns. Wright added these elements in 1911 to protect this exterior space and downplay its role as an entrance. At the same time, he added an automobile entrance to the south drive and removed the semicircular south veranda. The curved limestone cap stones (and probably the bricks) of this semicircular wall were relocated to an enclosed garden built west of the Studio's octagonal library. Wright's reuse of the limestone cap preserved it until 1985, when the cap was reinstalled atop the rebuilt south veranda.

Early emergency repairs included the installation of a new cedar-shingle roof, 1974. Photograph: Frank Lloyd Wright Preservation Trust.

West façade, c. 1925, showing the projecting trellis and columns that were added in 1911. The original semicircular veranda to the south has been removed. Photograph: Oak Park Public Library.

The large porch roof that had been added in 1911 masked the front (west façade) of the house. Its removal by a crew of volunteers in 1981 was the largest demolition project by the restoration committee before large-scale restoration began.

■ **VERANDA RECONSTRUCTION**

Reconstructing the circular sloping masonry wall of the southwestern veranda was one of the restoration's most complex projects. A plywood template of the original limestone cap was created, and a new concrete foundation was poured. The photograph (top right) shows the two-layered barrel-stave foundation formwork made out of Masonite, a flexible panel material.

The veranda common-brick masonry consists of two layers: the inner wall rises straight up, while the outer wall is sloped. The plywood templates and a trammel point were used to adjust the changing radii precisely. Finally, the capstones were settled on top.

Restored west façade of the Home, 2000. Photograph: Tim Long. Frank Lloyd Wright Preservation Trust.

■ RESTORED WEST FAÇADE

The 1889 front door was a Dutch (horizontally divided) door, but Wright replaced it in 1895 with the design seen here. The front door was re-created with its diamond-pane glass with lead cames and located in the southwest bay. The gable was completely reshingled. This project was used as a fundraising opportunity: donors were invited to sign their names on the backs of the cedar shingles before they were affixed to the building. The west façade of the Home eventually resembled its appearance in 1909 and included the following restorations:

- Lunette window re-created
- South veranda re-created
- Veranda on the west and north sides rebuilt
- Front steps and walkway re-created

- Entrance door rebuilt in the southwest bay
- Iron gate to veranda re-created
- All art-glass windows and sashes reconditioned
- Front yard landscape restored and re-created
- Driveway and walkways re-created
- Chicago Avenue wall re-created
- West façade reshingled

*Restored south façade of the Home, 1986.
Photograph: Jon Miller, Hedrich Blessing
Photographers.*

■ RESTORED SOUTH FAÇADE

The south façade of the Home was restored according to the 1889 construction drawings, historic photographs and David Wright's memories of the home. Before restoration, the brick wainscoting of the south elevation was painted red to match the red brick of the 1911 garage addition. The paint was chemically removed in 1985, and the original Chicago common brick was restained brown to match the rest of the house. When the Foundation obtained the property, the outside door to the kitchen had a wood porch that dated from 1911 to 1925. David Wright helped re-create the 1895 porch, which, according to his memory, was designed with spindled rails. He described the use of the south porch yard as an area where the wash was hung on a clothesline and pigeon and chicken coops lined the driveway. Ice, coal and milk were delivered to the back of the house. Concrete steps led down to the basement door. The photograph also shows the playroom's south bay window and the dining room bay to the left, with the dayroom bay directly above it.

The Home's front stairs seen from the living room, c. 1889–95. Photograph: The Frank Lloyd Wright Foundation, Scottsdale, Arizona.

ENTRY

■ FRONT STAIRS AND ENTRY HALL

In 1889 the entry hall was located at the southwest corner of the Home and led, through wide openings, to the living room and dining room. This photograph, dated 1889 to 1895, was one of the main sources the restoration architects used in re-creating the entry stairs. An article in an 1897 issue of *House Beautiful* described the entry hall as being "practically filled by the staircase."

In 1911, as Wright prepared to leave Oak Park, he moved the front door to the south side of the Home (adjacent to the driveway) as an automobile entrance with stairs on the interior leading up into the original entry hall. This prerestoration photograph shows the automobile entrance at grade level leading up to the entry hall.

Wright's home had a surprising amount of classical sculpture on display, in keeping with the practice of cultured people of the era to own reproductions of classical works to demonstrate that they were themselves "cultured."

The plaster frieze in the entry was installed when the house was originally built and has survived not only all of Wright's later remodelings but also the various "modernizations" that occurred between 1925 and the Foundation's acquisition of the building. Research indicated

Entry hall with the first restoration of the front stairs, 1986. Photograph: Jon Miller, Hedrich Blessing Photographers.

■ FIRST RESTORATION OF FRONT STAIRS

To restore the 1909 entry, the automobile entrance had to be removed and the foyer staircase leading up to the second floor had to be rebuilt. Historic photographs did not show the stairs distinctly, so the restoration architects based their final drawings on a combination of sources, including the 1889 construction drawings and studies of other period Wright houses. When complete, the expansive staircase cascaded into the entry hall as the 1897 magazine article had described, but it did not agree with David Wright's clear memory of it. His recollections raised the possibility that Wright had remodeled the stairs before 1909.

that P. P. Caproni and Brother of Boston, purveyors of plaster statuary and ornament, probably cast the frieze. It re-creates on a much smaller scale a portion of the Great Altar of Zeus at Pergamum, part of a Hellenistic temple complex in what is now Turkey. During the restoration of the Home, this entry frieze was cleaned and painted.

In both the Home and the Studio, Wright displayed other reproductions of classical sculpture, including his two favorites, the *Winged Victory* and the *Venus de Milo*. ■

Second restoration of the front stairs, 1999. Photograph: Tim Long. Frank Lloyd Wright Preservation Trust.

■ SECOND RESTORATION OF FRONT STAIRS

David Wright remembered much narrower stairs with a wood railing. He recalled grabbing onto the front post of the rail as he ran in the front door and up the stairs. He had clear memories of the children taking off their boots on a long bench along the south wall and putting them on the heating register opposite to dry. Further paint analysis during the restoration suggested that between 1905 and 1907, Wright had narrowed the stairs, lengthened the bench and added radiators near the front door to make more room for the busy activity in the entry hall and to help warm this cold area. David would have been about twelve. The restoration committee voted for a second restoration of the staircase based on this new evidence. The revised stairs, completed in 1991, can be seen in the photograph above.

The Home living room, 1890.
Photograph: Beautiful Homes and Social
Customs of America.

achieve the balance and repose he sought in his architecture. In time, he added furniture pieces of his own design. He also replaced some of the classical art with works by Midwestern artists, which he displayed in wide gilt-wood frames that he designed himself.

Architecturally, the living room was dominated by an octagonal bay window (the only source of natural light), and diagonally across the room in the opposite corner, a recessed fireplace inglenook. Plaster-covered beams and a dentil cornice grid the ceiling. Wright copied these from the second-floor lobby of the Auditorium Theatre, for which he drew most of the details when working for Adler & Sullivan.

The Foundation's paint analysis corroborated the description of the wall colors in the 1897 *House Beautiful* article—a deep olive-green dado (lower wall) and the color of "old sheepskin" on the upper walls. Horizontal oak trim at the window, door-top and dado height ran continuously throughout the living room, entry and dining room to link the spaces together—a detail found in East Coast Shingle-style houses from the 1870s as well as in period drawings of Japanese interiors.

Around 1895, Wright enlarged the living room by adding another half-octagonal bay and window seat to the north wall to meet the west (front) bay at the corner. This large wraparound bay became the precursor of Wright's trademark corner windows.

LIVING ROOM

■ HISTORIC LIVING ROOM

In his living room, as in the rest of his home, Wright tried out his interior design ideas. As this 1890 photograph shows, the eclectic decorating included oriental runners bought at auctions in Chicago, a bearskin rug, brocades and a bust of Beethoven (Wright's favorite composer). Wright would spend many a Saturday afternoon arranging furnishings and art objects to

Wright situated the hearth at the heart of his house, as he continued to do for his entire architectural career. The small inglenook created a private space in front of the fireplace. The hanging Japanese scroll, the Russian brass samovars and the oriental runners show Wright's interest in foreign decorative arts—an expression of his cultured taste in Victorian America.

Living room, looking south, prerestoration, 1975. Photograph: Frank Lloyd Wright Preservation Trust.

View of the inglenook, c. 1895–96. Photograph: The Frank Lloyd Wright Foundation, Scottsdale, Arizona.

■ BEFORE RESTORATION

On the top right is a view of the living room looking south, prior to restoration. Straight ahead is the entry. To the left is the inglenook, which had undergone no notable changes.

Before restoration, the north end of the living room still contained Wright's 1911 changes—the north bay window had been removed and the room extended into an alcove that occupied the entire north veranda.

North view of the living room after partial restoration, 1984. Photograph: Donald Kalec. Frank Lloyd Wright Preservation Trust.

North view of the living room during restoration, showing the framing of the north bay and window seat, 1986. Photograph: Frank Lloyd Wright Preservation Trust.

■ **DURING RESTORATION**

Here the north bay window and its built-in window seat are being rebuilt with quarter-sawn oak. In the top left corner can be seen an opening for a new steel beam to help support the living room ceiling joists. They were deflecting because the contractor, in 1889, had not installed them correctly per Wright's construction drawings.

Restored living room, 1986. Photograph: Jon Miller, Hedrich Blessing Photographers.

◼ RESTORED LIVING ROOM

With its ceiling patched, north bay and window benches re-created, walls plaster skim-coated to re-create the original sand finish and painted in historically correct colors, the living room returned to its appearance in 1909. The plaster ceiling beams and dentil cornice are original. Three of the four plaster corner ceiling panels are new casts from a single original panel that remained in the room. The armchairs, designed by Wright about 1893, are original to the Home, as are the print table (also a Wright design) used to display Japanese prints, and the carved wooden chest and the Chinese stool, both probably bought at auction by Wright. The built-in seating was upholstered with tufted green velvet cushions to match the original wall color. The painting on the back wall, *Wheatfields,* is a pastel rendering by Wright's artist friend, Charles Corwin.

Restored living room inglenook, 1986. Photograph: Jon Miller, Hedrich Blessing Photographers.

■ RESTORED INGLENOOK

To restore the inglenook to 1909, original plaster was patched and painted, and the built-in seats were re-covered with tufted green velvet. Portieres were re-created in the same fabric and hung as in the historic photographs. The mantel with its oak cabinets, the fireplace breast and the hearth are original. A mirror hung above the mantel was seen in historic photographs and also described in the 1897 *House Beautiful* article as reflecting light and "giving a most surprising result." It was reinstalled during the restoration.

The cabinets above the fireplace held decorative art objects and could be closed off when one wearied of looking at them. The motto "Truth Is Life" above the fireplace is a gentler version of Wright's family motto, "Truth Against the World." The inscription on the top-hinged door (concealing a shallow storage space) was added at a later time, but probably by Wright, who loved mottoes.

Another piece of original art is the landscape painting on the right by William Wendt, an American impressionist. It is framed in a reproduction of the original Wright-designed gilt-oak frame.

High openings on the north and south sides of the inglenook afford a peek into the adjacent study and dining room, adding to the sense of flowing space created by the open floor plan. The Wright children found their own uses for what they referred to as the "cozy corner." In an interview in 1975, Catherine Baxter, Catherine and Frank Lloyd Wright's oldest daughter, remembered holding hands with her boyfriend in the inglenook as a fourteen-year-old (1908). David Wright recalled shooting paper wads at his siblings through the openings.

Home study seen through the living room doorway, c. 1895–96. Photograph: The Frank Lloyd Wright Foundation, Scottsdale, Arizona.

Partially restored Home study, 1985. Photograph: Donald Kalec. Frank Lloyd Wright Preservation Trust.

HOME STUDY

■ HISTORIC HOME STUDY

The only historic photographs of the original dining room (later the study) are limited views from the living room. This photograph shows part of the room after 1895 when it was used as a study. A tall cabinet with a glazed door is built into one corner. A corresponding cabinet is in the opposite corner, to the left of the window. Between them, a cabinet at windowsill height provides even more storage. The ceiling light fixture is similar to ones in the living room and entry. On top of the tall cabinet is an American Indian figure, *Navaho Orator*, by Hermon Atkins MacNeil, the American sculptor who specialized in portraying the West. The children did their homework in the study, presumably at the "large heavy table" that "practically filled" the room, according to the 1897 *House Beautiful* article.

■ BEFORE RESTORATION

Prior to the major Home restoration of 1985, the study wood trim and cabinets were refinished, carpet removed, floor refinished, and the glazed doors on the tall cabinets replaced. The photograph shows the original bookcases and cabinets, which were not removed in any of Wright's remodelings. Paint analysis as well as the window frame confirmed that the original 1889 inset bay was removed and replaced by a straight wall with a band of new windows above eye level (seen here) in the 1911 remodeling by Wright. The windows ran up into a wide slot in the ceiling so their tops could not be seen. This spatial device gave the impression that the room was higher than it actually was and provided privacy for the occupants of the Studio, which was then made into a separate residence. The windows were returned to their 1889 configuration during the restoration.

Detail of the spatial device created by Wright in 1911 when he remodeled the Home study windows. Photograph: Donald Kalec. Frank Lloyd Wright Preservation Trust.

RECONSTRUCTING THE HOME STUDY WINDOWS

The reconstruction of the windows in the Home study is a good example of how difficult restoration decisions were made. Without photographic evidence showing the configuration of the windows in 1909, the restoration architects had to piece together multiple sources of information to re-create the historically correct windows.

When Wright added his studio in 1898, his studio office overlapped the exterior of the Home study at the northeast corner, blocking the eastern end window of the north wall.

Did Wright remodel the study wall to accommodate the blockage or just adapt the existing wall and bay window? A plan of the Studio published in the article "The Architect's Studio" in an 1899 issue of *House Beautiful* shows the study windows as straight, not bowed. In the same plan, the end window, now blocked by the addition of Wright's office, is shown as an interior window between the studio office and home study. Was this a preliminary plan, never executed, or the way the remodeling was done? Evidence from probing in and around the remains of the 1895 wall indicated that the window was still bowed, not straight, in 1909. The remaining framing, with its angled studs and shingles wrapping around the corner of the opening, was for a bowed window. Catherine Baxter also remembered the window as a bay.

The restoration architects determined that the blockage of the east angled window of the inset bay was taken care of by simply plastering over the former glass opening. The same treatment was given to the angled window on the opposite side, for balance. As the following photograph of the completely restored study shows, this was the configuration to which the windows were restored. ■

Restored Home study, 1986. Photograph: Jon Miller, Hedrich Blessing Photographers.

■ RESTORED HOME STUDY

The wall color of the study matches the green-gold of the living room, accentuating the "one-room" openness of Wright's floor plan. The door to the left opens onto the front veranda. Most of the woodwork is original, including the buffet. The restoration architects used the inside of one of the base cabinet doors as the "control" for matching all the "golden oak" stain in the rest of the Home. Stain analysis proved that the back of this door had never faded or been restained since its first coat in 1889–90.

The table seen here is a Wright design but was not used in his home. It is on loan from the University of Illinois at Chicago. The Foundation obtained two slant-back chairs (c. 1903) that were originally designed by Wright for the employees' dining room at the Larkin Company in Buffalo, New York, but that had been used in various rooms in the Home. Two more chairs were reproduced. The room also houses a built-in octagonal-front china cabinet (not shown here) reproduced from historic photographs and probes that revealed how the original cabinet was fixed to the wall.

DINING ROOM

■ **1895–1898**

In 1895, Frank Lloyd Wright converted the 1889 kitchen of his home to a dining room and enlarged it by adding a wider octagonal bay to the south end. He strove to make this room a total environment—his first—that integrated architecture, interior design, furniture, decorative arts, and built-in lighting and heating. He used simple and natural materials: red terra-cotta tile laid in a basket-weave pattern on the floor and fireplace front, a warm golden-brown linen covering the walls, and honey-colored oak woodwork

and furniture. The dining table and chairs were among Wright's first furniture designs, the high backs of the chairs creating an intimate room-within-a-room feeling. Not seen in this photograph is a built-in ceiling light covered with a fretwork panel.

The octagonal bay, with its tall lotus-pattern art-glass windows on five sides, formed a ribbon of light around a deep, low platform in the bay that probably held potted plants—a conservatory end facing south. Art objects lined the window ledges. At the opposite end, Wright added a tile-fronted fireplace where the kitchen stove had been.

In 1897, when the house to the south was built tight against the lot line, Wright removed a platform from the south bay and filled in the lower portion of the windows to afford privacy. This 1897–98 photograph shows these modifications. It was this appearance to which the room was restored.

Dining room, view looking south, c. 1911–25. Photograph: Henry Fuermann. Avery Architectural and Fine Arts Library, Columbia University in the City of New York.

Dining room prior to restoration, c. 1974. Photograph: Frank Lloyd Wright Preservation Trust.

■ 1911 MODIFICATIONS

When Wright converted the Home into a rental property in 1911, he added two cantilevered lights in the bay end of the dining room. He removed the counters below the full-height windows on each side so that the space could be used for chairs when they were not needed at the table. The room remained largely in this state until the Foundation acquired the Home and Studio. This historic photograph shows the clearest view of the ceiling grille.

■ BEFORE RESTORATION

The dining room was in poor condition. The previous owner had begun restoring it but stopped at stripping the woodwork and removing all the wall-paper down to the cracked and patched plaster. The room also required some structural repairs. The added bay end had settled as much as 1.5 inches in some areas. Since the room could be worked on without impinging on the rest of the building and the funds for restoring this limited area could be raised relatively easily, the restoration committee decided to tackle the work in the dining room as its first complete restoration project.

To bring the floor back to level, the wood framing of the bay end was jacked up slowly to minimize plaster cracking in the bay (on the first and second floors). The floor framing was strengthened and leveled by attaching new joists to each side of the original ones.

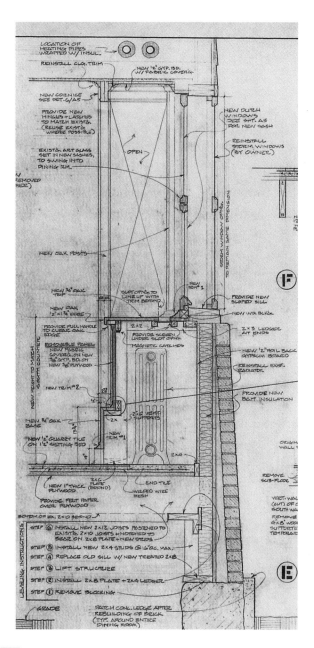

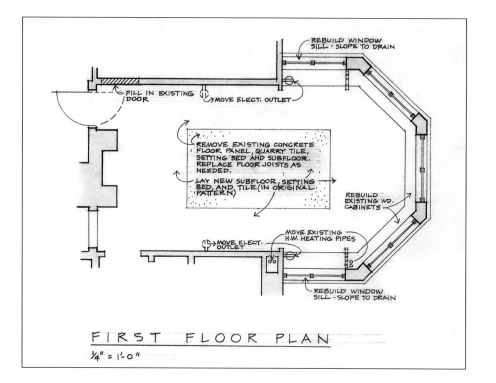

Dining room cabinet and exterior wall detail. Construction drawing. *As in every room, specific construction drawings were made for each part of the dining room restoration. Here is a detail showing a section through the dining room radiator cabinets and exterior wall. Drawing: Donald Kalec. Photograph: Frank Lloyd Wright Preservation Trust.*

Dining room design drawing. *An example of a design/scope-of-work drawing prepared by the restoration committee to guide the restoration architect in his preparation of construction drawings for the dining room restoration. Drawing: Donald Kalec. Photograph: Frank Lloyd Wright Preservation Trust.*

■ DURING RESTORATION

The original art-glass windows were carefully packed and stored during the restoration of the dining room. Whenever possible, original materials (such as the wood trim and floor tiles) were carefully removed, cleaned and reinstalled. As in every other part of the building, new electrical wiring (to meet electrical code) was carefully threaded through walls and ceilings to preserve the original plaster. The new wiring for the built-in ceiling light can be seen in the ceiling cove (facing page). A decorative wood grille eventually hid the light sockets and electrical conduit from view.

The tile in the center of the dining room floor had been replaced by a concrete slab. Probably when Wright remodeled the Home in 1911 as a rental unit, he wanted tile to replace the wood floor in the bay end (which had never been tiled because a platform had been there in 1895). He obtained the tiles by removing them from the middle of the floor and installing a rectangular concrete fill in their place. By 1977 the tile floor was in poor condition. The base was breaking up and the tiles were coming loose. The only solution was to take up the tiles, remove the base and start over. These tiles are no longer made, so every effort was extended to preserve and reuse as many as possible, even ones that were chipped or cracked.

Once the subfloor had been made level, a combination of original and replacement tiles (cut to size from stock modern tiles) was laid in the original basket-weave pattern. A skilled tile setter inserted the pieces over a 2-inch-thick "mud" or dry concrete bed, using the historically accurate way of laying a tile floor, in contrast to the thin-set method used today. A double row of thin black tiles bordered the floor on the sides of the room. Since the room was out of square, the tile setter worked from a center line using a gridded board to make sure the pattern did not expand or contract as he worked out from the center. The spaces between the tiles were minuscule, leaving no room for error. The slight color difference between the old and new tile is in conformity with current restoration practice, so the original fabric can be discerned in a subtle way that does not distract from the overall effect.

The dining room restoration in progress, 1977. Photograph: Frank Lloyd Wright Preservation Trust.

To restore the dining room's tile floor, the tiles were carefully removed and cleaned before being reinstalled, 1977. Photograph: Frank Lloyd Wright Preservation Trust.

The tile floor was reinstalled using a historically accurate method and a combination of original and replacement tiles, 1977. Photograph: Frank Lloyd Wright Preservation Trust.

Detail of the dining room photograph from which the lighting grille pattern was re-created, c. 1919–25. Photograph: Henry Fuermann. Avery Architectural and Fine Arts Library, Columbia University in the City of New York.

Samples of the fabric that originally covered the dining room walls were found beneath wood trim, 1977. Photograph: Frank Lloyd Wright Preservation Trust.

■ DECORATIVE FEATURES

One of the most perplexing problems facing the restoration committee was determining what kind of cloth Wright had used to cover the dining room walls and ceiling. Research had unearthed some small fragments of fabric from behind pieces of trim, but the committee spent almost two years trying to determine what the fabric was and where it could be obtained. Replacement fabric was compared to the samples for weight and weave and then dyed to match the center portion of the original samples since that area had been protected best by the trim.

Electricity had been available for homes in Oak Park beginning about 1901. Wright had anticipated this and had his home wired when it was built in 1889. By the time the dining room addition was constructed, electricity had been in common use in Oak Park for only four years. Wright seized upon the creative possibilities the new technology presented. Historic photographs of the room showed that in the ceiling above the dining room table, Wright designed and installed an elaborate oak, fretsawn light grille with a pattern of stylized oak leaves and geometric forms. This was his first use of recessed, indirect lighting, and one of the first examples anywhere. Nothing but the empty frame of this grille and the recess behind it, with fluorescent lighting, remained when the Foundation acquired the property.

Using the historic photograph, which showed only part of the grille, as a guide, a full-size pattern of one-quarter of the grille was drawn. It was replicated three times to form the four identical quadrants of the whole 8 foot 5-inch x 4 foot .05-inch grille design. This grille drawing was then spray-glued on a high grade of quarter-inch oak plywood as a template for the carver.

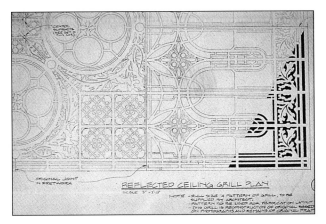

Re-created template of the dining room ceiling grille, 1977. Photograph: Frank Lloyd Wright Preservation Trust.

Woodworker Major Kassiah cutting the intricate grille pattern, 1977. Photograph: Frank Lloyd Wright Preservation Trust.

The rich glow from the dining room's built-in ceiling light testifies to Wright's success in creatively experimenting with electric lighting, 1977. Photograph: Frank Lloyd Wright Preservation Trust.

A talented woodworker carefully fabricated each of the four panels that make up the grille. Each panel was cut separately with a jigsaw so that there were fresh, exact cuts in each section. The original would have been done with a fretsaw, a narrow-bladed, fine-toothed saw held under tension in a frame and used for cutting curved outlines.

The existing grille frame gave clues as to how the grille had been set up. Wright had placed a layer of rice paper between the grille and the lightbulbs, allowing a diffused light to filter through the grille pattern onto the table. The restoration architects divided the frame into eleven sections and placed a lightbulb in each so that there would be no shadows within the fretwork. In compliance with fire safety requirements, the rice paper was replaced with a translucent sheet of fiberglass. The whole re-created grille is attached by hinges and swings open to facilitate cleaning and changing the lightbulbs.

We knew from Wright's description that there had been some kind of fabric wall covering and we found a piece on the back of some trim, but we couldn't find a manufactured cloth that matched the color and weave of the old sample. We completed the rest of the room and painted the walls the historically correct brown so the room looked finished. Finally, one of the restoration committee members suggested boiling the samples to remove the glue in them. Soon after that he came in one day with an old oil painting. Turning it over we saw that it had been painted on the same fabric as was used in the dining room. The fabric Wright used was painter's linen. Looking in art supply catalogs, we eventually found a painter's linen that was almost identical in weave, and had it dyed to match. A backing was then applied. Each process had to be done by different companies in different parts of the country. Altogether, the fabric took twice as long as the rest of the room. ∎

—Donald Kalec
Director of research and restoration, 1981–86

69

DINING CHAIRS

The dining room chairs are the seminal design for the tall-backed chairs that Wright became famous for designing for many clients. The original chairs were still in existence. Catherine Wright took them with her when she moved out in 1918, and they were eventually passed on to Llewellyn Wright. He gave them back to his father in 1953 when he moved into a house designed for him by Frank Lloyd Wright. The chairs were still at Taliesin, Wright's home in Wisconsin, when the restoration began. The restoration committee wrote to Olgivanna Wright, Frank Lloyd Wright's widow, then president of The Frank Lloyd Wright Foundation, requesting that she loan six original dining chairs to the Home and Studio Foundation. Mrs. Wright generously agreed to donate the chairs rather than just lending them. She felt that they belonged in their original location. Several years later, The Frank Lloyd Wright Foundation agreed to provide the two remaining dining room chairs to the Frank Lloyd Wright Home and Studio Foundation as a long-term loan. ■

Dining chair. Designed by Frank Lloyd Wright. Gift of Olgivanna Wright. Photograph: Philip Mrozinski. Frank Lloyd Wright Preservation Trust.

■ RESTORED DINING ROOM

Family meals were *de rigeur* in the Wright household, as in all middle-class American homes at that time. Even the youngest child, Llewellyn, had a place at the table. The high chair, seen in the background (facing page), was designed for him by his father. The dining room table, designed by Wright, was one of three tables used in the room at various times. It was purchased from the estate of sculptor Alfonso Ianelli, who had collaborated with Wright on the elaborate Midway Gardens project in the 1920s.

The dining room restoration re-created one of Frank Lloyd Wright's most complete early spaces. The room displays many of the important aesthetic traits of Wright's Prairie-style work: natural materials, earth-toned colors and furniture integrated with architecture.

Following Wright's scheme to integrate mechanical services into the archi-

View of the restored dining room, looking toward the tile-fronted fireplace, 1999. Photograph: Roger Straus III, Roger and Doris Straus Photography.

South view of the restored dining room, 1999. Photograph: Tim Long. Frank Lloyd Wright Preservation Trust.

tecture, the original built-in cabinets in the bay end conceal hot-water radiators. Slots at floor level and along the cabinet tops allow for air circulation.

This model project took almost a year and was funded with a combination of government and private grants. Its successful completion provided a springboard for other funding opportunities. The strategies for restoration planning that were successfully tested in the dining room were subsequently followed in the rest of the building.

71

*Restored kitchen, 1986. Photograph: John Miller,
Hedrich Blessing Photographers.*

KITCHEN

The restoration committee never found a historic photograph of the kitchen, probably because kitchens, then the domain of servants, were not often photographed. A new kitchen was the major part of the service wing added on the back (east) of the Home c. 1895. A passageway connected the kitchen with the pantry and had an outside back door to which ice was delivered. Coal for the furnace was delivered directly through the basement window. Two casement windows on each side of the kitchen helped cool the room when the cast-iron stove, stoked with wood or coal, and later gas, was in use. The Wrights had a cook, and the children were instructed to keep out of her way. The temptation must have been great, however, because the back stairs, leading to the playroom, came close by the kitchen.

The kitchen restoration was based on a 1985 interview with David Wright and on plan sketches made by John Lloyd Wright in 1925 when he was trying to sell the property for his father. The restoration was a labor of love for many volunteers. One volunteer doggedly researched the type of stove needed and possible sources. He found what he was looking for —"a coal- and wood-burning stove with a gas-fired attachment"—at the Good Time Stove Company in Goshen, Massachusetts. The sink, table, chairs and lighting fixtures are of the period. The cabinets are reproductions with architectural salvage hardware. Historic pots, pans and other kitchen utensils were donated or loaned by many of the Foundation's supporters. Some years later, a period icebox was added to the kitchen.

PANTRY

In 1889, the pantry was located between the original kitchen and dining room. Filled from floor to ceiling with built-in cabinets, drawers and shelves, it was typical for the period. The pantry was enlarged in 1895 when the service wing was added to the rear (east) of the Home. A sink was installed in the extension, probably to wash the dishes that were stored in the pantry. Even though the original kitchen was remodeled as a dining room at the same time, the pantry continued its use as a service area because it was still adjacent to the dining room and to the corridor leading to the kitchen. In the 1950s and 1960s, the pantry was used as a kitchen in the first-floor apartment. As was the case with the original kitchen, no historic photographs of the pantry were available.

Restoration projects in the pantry included reinforcing and replastering the ceiling and skim-coating the walls to match the original texture. The maple floors were stripped and refinished. The cabinets seen here are original. Others, on the north side of the room, were re-created based on Wright's original 1889 plans. The radiator is probably original to the installation of the hot-water heating system c. 1901. Limoges china (used for formal occasions) and silver flatware belonging to the Wright family were donated by family members and are displayed in the cabinets, as are Blue Willow dishes similar to the family's everyday china.

Restored pantry, looking west, 1986. Photograph: Jon Miller, Hedrich Blessing Photographers.

When Frank and Catherine's fourth child, David, was born in 1895, they realized that their little cottage was bursting—the two oldest boys, Lloyd and John, filled the nursery, and their daughter, Catherine, nearly two, almost certainly was still in the master bedroom. Besides adding a larger dining room, a new kitchen, and a playroom for the children, Wright solved the shortage of bedrooms by converting his studio into a quasi-dormitory for the older children. Wright built a head-high partition down the middle, creating one sleeping area for the girls and another for the boys. In 1911, when Wright made the Home into a rental unit, this partition was removed and the shallow cabinets on each side were replaced by deeper built-in wardrobes, drawer units and a dressing table. Two small dormers were added on the sides for cross ventilation. No historic photograph of this room has been found.

To re-create the 1909 appearance, the restoration committee had to plan to remove the later wardrobes and drawer units and re-create the original shallow cabinets as well as divide the room with a partition to re-create the children's bedrooms. Remembering the pillow fights that took place over it, David Wright judged the height of the partition to be approximately seven feet. The partition, although historically accurate, diminished the dramatic impact of the room, and many volunteers regretted the necessity of reconstructing it. Historical accuracy, however, won out.

STUDIO/CHILDREN'S ROOMS

■ BEFORE AND DURING RESTORATION

Fitted under the space of the Home's expansive western gable was Wright's studio, which had a high vaulted ceiling and a band of six windows topped with a semicircular (lunette) window that looked out onto the front yard and Forest Avenue. Shallow built-in cabinets lined both sides of the room. This room (and the master bedroom) went up underneath the high-pitched gable, making Wright's workroom the most spacious in the Home. It was here that Wright drew up the Charnley House (Chicago, 1891) at night for his employer Louis Sullivan, for extra pay—and then went on to "moonlight" by designing houses for his own clients.

Restored girls' and boys' bedrooms, 1986. Photograph: Jon Miller, Hedrich Blessing Photographers.

■ **RESTORED CHILDREN'S BEDROOMS**

The rebuilt partition re-created the girls' and boys' bedrooms with a shared lunette window. The restoration architects were able to preserve most of the original wood trim. Wall sconces were re-created from photographs and measurements of existing fixtures. The closets are reproductions based on historic photographs and markings found on the floor. The bed in the girls' room was designed by Wright for the Avery Coonley House (Riverside, Illinois, 1907). The table in the boys' room was also designed by Wright, for the Mori oriental art store.

Master bedroom, looking south, c. 1895–1905. The photographer was possibly Frank Lloyd Wright. Photograph: The Frank Lloyd Wright Foundation, Scottsdale, Arizona.

MASTER BEDROOM

■ HISTORIC MASTER BEDROOM

The master bedroom was noted on the 1889 construction plans as a "chamber" (short for "bedchamber"). Its ceiling, emphasized by wood trim, reaches up into what normally would have been attic area, giving this modest-sized room an air of spaciousness. Both end walls have complex compositions made up of mural paintings, hanging light fixtures and (on the north end) windows. The two dressing closets, curtained off rather than with doors, would have been unusual for such a modest house in 1889. Each had drawers and shelves for storing clothes (the wire clothes hanger had not yet been invented). Painted on both end walls are Native American figures by Wright's friend, the painter and designer Orlando Giannini. The frieze on the side walls is a metallic-gold stencil pattern similar to one found in Louis Sullivan's Auditorium Building. Paint analysis during restoration indicated that the murals in this bedroom were painted later (c. 1904) than the frieze was stenciled. The basswood floor was stained a reddish brown. Through the door on the left can be seen the wood-paneled bathroom. While the rest of the Home uses oak for all the trim and cabinets, the master bedroom uses birch, even for the sides of the doors facing the room. (The other sides, facing the hall and bath, are oak). It was quite common for second-floor rooms, especially bedrooms, to feature a different wood than the rest of the house.

Master bedroom before restoration, 1985.
Photograph: Frank Lloyd Wright Preservation Trust.

Master bedroom during restoration; the mural area on the south wall is covered with protective tissue, 1986. Photograph: Frank Lloyd Wright Preservation Trust.

■ BEFORE AND DURING RESTORATION

Prior to restoration, the master bedroom still had its vaulted ceiling accentuated by birch trim and its original closets, but the decorative details that had made this Frank and Catherine's elegant private retreat were either gone or hidden. From 1984 to 1986, while restoring the interior of the Studio, the Foundation used this room as a drafting room.

For a period of time between 1925 and 1974 when the building was subdivided into rental apartments, the master bedroom became the kitchen for the upstairs unit. Water leaking from a 1911 dormer and perhaps humidity from the kitchen caused serious damage to the plaster walls. The restoration committee stripped the room down to the wood lath and completely replastered. They knew from photographic evidence and paint analysis that the two murals by Orlando Giannini were still in the upper part of the room under eight coats of paint. Tissue paper was applied to the murals with water-soluble paste to protect them during the surrounding plaster removal. It took three paint conservators three months to uncover and conserve the hidden Giannini murals.

■ BEDROOM MURALS

The finish coat of plaster was pulling away from the base coat, requiring it to be stabilized. In a painstaking and time-consuming process, a plaster specialist used hypodermic needles filled with an adhesive mixture and injected approximately every 2 square inches of the wall.

Small bottle jacks were placed between the mural plaster and a backboard. As the moisture in the adhesive softened the plaster overnight, the pressure from the jacks flattened it. As the finish coat of plaster dried, it once again adhered to the base coat.

After the plaster was stabilized, eight layers of paint were carefully removed. On the south wall, this was accomplished by meticulous removal with scalpels; on the north wall, a chemical solution was used. The murals were cleaned, coated with a clear material that allows for correction of any errors in the future and then in-painted where necessary.

The murals that emerged after conservation depicted strong figures of the soil looking somewhat like Native Americans, a subject of interest to both Wright and Giannini. Their Egyptian-looking garments are perhaps

The partially restored Giannini mural on the master bedroom's south wall, 1986. Photograph: Frank Lloyd Wright Preservation Trust.

Artists painted in sections to restore the Giannini murals, 1986. Photograph: Frank Lloyd Wright Preservation Trust.

An artist re-created the stencil pattern on the walls of the master bedroom, 1986. Photograph: Frank Lloyd Wright Preservation Trust.

accounted for by the popularity of Egyptology at the turn of the century. Paintings by Orlando Giannini show a blend of American and Near East Indian figures in exotic costumes performing mysterious rituals.

Like the murals, the Sullivanesque stencil patterns had been covered over with coats of paint. Because of the extreme deterioration of the plaster in these areas, the restoration committee decided to have the stencils re-created on the walls rather than attempting to uncover and conserve the originals.

■ RESTORED MASTER BEDROOM

With the Giannini murals conserved and authentic furnishings installed, Wright's master bedroom was returned to its 1909 splendor. The delicate pendant globes, known as "stalactite lights," were quite common but virtually unobtainable now in such a large size and the number needed. The answer was for them to be hand-blown by a glass artist. The re-creation of the plaster medallions from which they hang resulted from a serendipitous discovery. One of the original plaster medallions was found during the wall rebuilding, resting inside the stud space. From this artifact, which matched the medallions in historic photographs, the committee was able to have reproductions cast. Wright's original birch double bed had been burned in a fire while in storage at the home of one of his family members, so a replica was created for the room based on historic photographs. On the exterior, a later balcony was removed and replaced with the smaller 1909 version.

In the nursery/dayroom—Catherine Tobin Wright with Lloyd (perched next to her), John (on the floor) and Catherine (in the Tobin family spool crib), c. 1895. Photograph: Frank Lloyd Wright Preservation Trust.

NURSERY/DAYROOM

■ HISTORIC DAYROOM

When the children moved into the former studio, the nursery became Catherine's dayroom. Here, Catherine tended to the children, read and sewed. In a 1975 interview, Catherine Baxter referred to the room as "a gathering place for all of us and a haven when troubled waters rose to submerge us."

The bay area (with its lowered ceiling) was built in 1895 when the bay was added to the dining room below. The photograph shows three sets of diamond-pane windows in the bay area. The center sash was filled in after the house to the south was built in 1897. Possibly at the same time, Wright added a clerestory window to make up for the loss of light. Note the closets on the sides that project out into the room for more depth. One of them contained a sink.

A small portion of an early stencil pattern was re-created in the corner behind the door to the dayroom, 1986. Photograph: Donald Kalec.

Detail of an early Sullivanesque stencil pattern still extant above the playroom hall ceiling. The same pattern decorated the upper walls of the dayroom, c. 1889. 1987. Photograph: Donald Kalec.

■ DURING RESTORATION

During restoration of the dayroom, when layers of wallpaper were removed, faint markings of a decorative stencil pattern dating from about 1889 were discovered around the upper walls. Untouched sections of the frieze are still extant above the playroom hall ceiling. From this the restoration committee made a new stencil and copied the original colors (silver on light green) onto a small section of the dayroom wall to show the contrast between the earlier decor and the clean, simple lines Wright had created by 1909. The rest of the walls were covered in plain off-white fabric to match the remnants found behind the trim.

The dayroom, restored to 1909, shows a long clerestory window that was added after 1895 between the two ceiling heights. Sunlight streams in from this southern exposure, giving the room a light, airy feel. Reproduction built-in cabinets conceal the radiators below the bay windows. The spool crib belonged to the Tobin family. Catherine Wright had been in it as a baby and used it for her own six children. It was returned to the Oak Park Home by the Tobin family. In keeping with the Foundation's collections policy of displaying other Wright-designed furniture of the period when furniture original to the Home is nonextant, this room also houses a high-backed chair designed for Wright's B. Harley Bradley House (Kankakee, Illinois, 1900) and a rocker from the Frederick C. Robie House (Chicago, 1910).

Restored dayroom, 1986. Photograph: Jon Miller, Hedrich Blessing Photographers.

Fortunately for us, either due to his tight budget or his own impatience to see results or attachment to his own work, Wright almost never removed anything, but instead built directly on top of it. When we removed the [1911] firewall from in front of the Home bathroom, we found a 1909 [window bay] bricked over on one side, plastered over on the other. The glass in the sash was broken and [a] new piece of glass was leaning next to it, [in the blocked-off bay]. Evidently Wright decided not to repair it, but just to brick it over, leaving the whole thing hidden and undisturbed for the next seventy-five years. ■

—Ann Abernathy, project architect
"Outline: Restoration Alternatives, Goals and Procedures," 1985

Restored bathroom, 1986. Photograph: Jon Miller, Hedrich Blessing Photographers.

BATHROOM

Archaeological probes indicated that Wright had remodeled the bathroom during the playroom addition of 1895 and again in 1911. The historic photograph (page 76) of the master bedroom (c. 1895–1905) was the only one that provided a view of the bathroom with its unusual board-and-batten walls. Catherine Baxter remembered in a 1977 interview that there were "pine boards in the bathroom," and she had always wanted tile like she saw in the homes of her friends. A piece of the batten was found between the joists during demolition of the floor, and the paneling was re-created for restoration to 1909. Placement of the bathtub, toilet and sink was determined by the pipe arrangement and notches in the studs. Exposed pipes and fittings were replated with nickel. Catalogs of the period guided the selection of the tub, sink and fittings, which were acquired from an architectural salvage company. The toilet, dated 1892, is original to the house, and was found in the basement.

During the course of the restoration, it was discovered that there had been a window on the north side of the room near the sink. This window was plastered over on one side and bricked over on the other during the 1911 remodeling. To compensate for the loss of the window, Wright had added a skylight, the light shaft of which projected into the playroom's barrel-vaulted ceiling. The restoration architects removed the skylight, restored the window and plastered the ceiling to return the bathroom to what it looked like in 1909.

PLAYROOM

■ HISTORIC PLAYROOM

On the second floor of the Home's 1895 wing, Wright designed one of his most delightful spaces: a playroom for his children. Below the barrel-vaulted ceiling with its arched wood bands, a wide, continuous wood shelf ran around the room. Wright lined the walls with brown Roman bricks, his first use of brick as an interior wall material—until then, he had used brick solely on exteriors.

Above a large Roman brick fireplace, a mural painted by Orlando Giannini depicted a scene from "The Fisherman and the Genie" from *The Arabian Nights,* one of the children's favorite stories.

Soft light filtered in through a skylight grille sawn into a geometric pattern inspired by the prickly ash tree. Along the north and south walls, art-glass bay windows let in sunlight, which cast geometric patterns on the wide expanse of oak floor. At night, brass electric fixtures along the sides provided light, and glass globes in differing sizes, lit by tiny bulbs, twinkled playfully as they hung in a cluster from the ceiling.

At the opposite end, Wright visually extended the room by stretching the barrel vault into the attic space. This upper area became a multilevel gallery for the Wright children to stage plays or to seat their audience.

The *Winged Victory,* one of Wright's favorite classical sculptures, and Japanese prints provided inspiration for the children. In this room, Catherine also ran a Froebel kindergarten and the Wrights entertained their friends. During this time there was a large double circle with twin cross bars painted on the floor as part of the Froebel play activities. Wright used this motif, a cross within a circle, in his professional logo during his Prairie years.

East view of playroom, undated photograph. House Beautiful, *February 1897.*

West view of playroom, pre-1905. Photograph by Frank Lloyd Wright. Avery Architectural and Fine Arts Library, Columbia University, New York City.

Prerestoration view of the playroom, facing east, c. 1974–82. Photograph: Frank Lloyd Wright Preservation Trust.

Prerestoration view of the playroom, facing west, 1975. Photograph: Frank Lloyd Wright Preservation Trust.

Detail of light shaft cutting through the playroom balcony, 1982. Photograph: Frank Lloyd Wright Preservation Trust.

■ BEFORE AND DURING RESTORATION

As part of his remodeling in 1911, Wright had closed up the north bay windows overlooking the Studio to secure privacy for his family, who would be moving there from the Home. He had also removed the built-in benches from the bays and a built-in grand piano. When the Foundation acquired the Home and Studio in 1974, the playroom's decorative ceiling grilles, as well as art-glass windows, were missing and the bookcases had lost their doors. However, Wright's Japanese-inspired cantilevered lights from 1906 had been preserved in the room's four corners. The Giannini mural in the playroom had never been painted over, so it needed less dramatic conservation than the ones in the master bedroom. However, a leak in the chimney had caused

a large piece of the plaster to come loose. After the chimney was repaired, a conservator secured the plaster and a painting specialist carefully removed some in-painting that had been done by a former owner. A semicircular band around the outside of the mural was repainted, and the entire mural was cleaned and coated with a protective layer.

Cutting into the playroom balcony ceiling on the right was the light shaft from Wright's 1911 remodeling of the adjacent bathroom. It was removed in order to restore the barrel vault over the attic stairs to its 1909 appearance. The color of the playroom walls was determined by dating the paint layers on the 1911 light shaft. The original coat of paint on the light shaft

Replica of the original playroom ceiling grille being created with period hand tools, 1982. Photograph: Frank Lloyd Wright Preservation Trust.

(1911) corresponded to a paint layer on the playroom walls and ceiling. The layer of wall and ceiling paint just beneath the 1911 color was what was there in 1909 in the playroom: an earthy gold.

The playroom's skylight was covered on the interior by four wood fretwork grilles that conformed to the curve of the barrel-vaulted ceiling. Only the curved frame remained by 1974. The grille design was drawn using a historic photograph as a reference. A skilled Wisconsin woodworker first bent the 3/16-inch oak veneer plywood to fit onto the original curved frame and then cut the fretwork using turn-of-the-century hand tools; the process involved about a year and a half for the four grilles to be made. Electric lighting above the grilles (but below the skylight) was rewired, and period reflectors were installed to re-create the same lighting effect at night—warm incandescent light filtering down through the stylized prickly ash leaves—as the Wright family would have enjoyed.

The re-created ceiling grille panels were installed in the original curved frame. As in the dining room's ceiling grille, translucent fiberglass rather than rice paper was used on the back of the panels. Above the frame (as seen in the photograph on right) are the light sources: a weather skylight and electric lights.

Installation of the playroom ceiling grille, 1982. Photograph: Frank Lloyd Wright Preservation Trust.

A completed panel of the playroom's ceiling grille leans against shelves of hand tools used in the grille-fabricating process. The entire grille is composed of sixteen identical geometric patterns in four panels, 1982. Photograph: Frank Lloyd Wright Preservation Trust.

FABRICATING THE PLAYROOM CEILING GRILLE

Experimenting with a photocopy of the geometric pattern, I tried to figure out the best way to transfer the design from the paper onto the wood. I decided it was best to tape the paper onto the wood and cut out the pattern with a razor-sharp chisel or gouge. It took several evenings of practice to determine the right amount of pressure which would cut through the paper and score the veneer, but not crush it. . . . After the pattern was scored, drill holes were used to remove waste.

. . . The larger waste areas would have to be cut away. I experimented with all-direction blades in my antique Roger's treadle jigsaw. It didn't work well. The 30.5 X 64-inch piece would be too big to manipulate for such small detail. After looking through an antique tool book, I saw a deep-throated fret saw and decided to make one using blades that would rotate. After making the saw and practicing, it seemed to give the control that I felt I needed. . . . I also made a flooring saw by rounding off the corner on a slotting saw and cutting new teeth with a Japanese feather file. It took about two weeks to prepare the tools. ■

—Mark Duginske
"Restoring Wright's 1895 Skylight," 1983

■ PLAYROOM WINDOWS

In 1909 the playroom contained fourteen art-glass windows in the bays on the north and south sides of the room. This glass, a stylized tulip design, was actually the second set of art glass for the bay windows. (In 1895, when the playroom was built, the art glass in the bays matched that of the bookcase doors—a large panel of clear glass surrounded by a border of small squares of clear glass.) When Wright separated the Home from the Studio in 1911, he removed the seven art-glass windows on the north side of the playroom and filled in the openings as part of a firewall installation that was required by Oak Park's building code. The restoration committee discovered that the glass from five of the windows had been reused by Wright in the apartment above the garage.

The windows were removed from the garage and turned over to an art-glass craftsman who carefully reset the glass in new brass-plated zinc cames. These five windows were installed in the restored north bay along with two reproduction windows crafted by the same glass artist.

The north and south bay window seats, which also doubled as toy boxes, were rebuilt as part of the restoration process. Their lids are not on top, but on the faces, bookcase style. Since the seats were prefabricated in the shop and would not fit up the stairs, they were hoisted in through the south bay with extreme care and put into place.

89

The playroom's grand piano was installed in an opening under the balcony stairs, just as Wright had done, 1982. Photograph: Frank Lloyd Wright Preservation Trust.

The piano recess with the original hook from which the piano was suspended, 1977. Photograph: Frank Lloyd Wright Preservation Trust.

■ PLAYROOM PIANO

Music was a critical influence on Frank Lloyd Wright and an important part of his children's education. One of the most exciting surprises of the restoration was finding a large iron hook in the back stairwell. Historic photographs did not explain the hook, but the committee learned from the Wright children that it had been used by Wright to suspend the back end of a grand piano after removing the back leg! He had devised this scheme so that only the keyboard and front legs were in the playroom. The rest of the instrument "floated" above the back stairs, held up by the wall hook, so the rear leg could be removed and not be an obstacle to anyone using the back stairs right under the piano.

The in-fill wall was removed and a donated grand piano, c. 1909, was acquired. It would not fit around the corner of the front stairs, so the movers brought it to the playroom up the back stairway and then inserted it backward into the opening under the upper gallery stairs. Like its predecessor, the piano is suspended from the original hook. Wright had hinges on the stair treads and landing leading to the playroom gallery to open and allow the sound to escape, filling both floors of the Home with the music.

We discovered the hook for the piano while probing under the trapdoor in the balcony stairway of the playroom. We put a flashlight in the cavity and it was like discovering a cave. We were incredulous about what we'd found—there was a long iron strap coming down with a big hook on the end, original paint on the walls and pieces of the wall fabric still there. We immediately tore out the later ceiling below and put the new discoveries on the tour. ■

—John G. Thorpe AIA
Restoration committee chairman

East view of the restored playroom, 1999. Photograph: Tim Long. Frank Lloyd Wright Preservation Trust.

■ RESTORED PLAYROOM

This view of the playroom from its balcony shows the wondrous space returned to its former glory. New glass doors were fabricated for the fireplace cabinets. With their pattern of small squares around a rectangle, they match the inset windows by the cantilevered light fixtures. Restoration is an ongoing process for the Frank Lloyd Wright Preservation Trust. In 1999 a set of original glass doors from the sides of the playroom bookcases was acquired through an auction.

As in the rest of the Home, period cast-iron hot-air floor registers were acquired at architectural salvage yards to closely match one original found in the building.

A Caproni cast of a bust of *Venus de Milo* sits on the mantel, in accordance with information from historic photographs. The unique Wright-designed light fixtures were cleaned and repaired as needed, using the original glass, cames and oak brackets.

To accommodate the building's state-of-the-art climate control system, hot-air supply slots were discreetly installed at the rear of the built-in toy benches. Unobtrusive return air slots were arranged on each side of the skylight grilles.

Restored playroom, looking west, 1986. Photograph: Jon Miller, Hedrich Blessing Photographers.

The restoration committee also acquired a Cecilian piano player which family members recalled was used often at social functions in the playroom. John Lloyd Wright wrote about it in his *My Father Who Is on Earth* (1994):

> One day, without previous warning at least to me, a Cecilian piano player was rolled into our house. Papa pushed it up to the keyboard of his Steinway concert grand and pumped Beethoven by the roll. His eyes closed, his head and hands swaying over the throttles, I think he imagined he was Beethoven. He looked like Beethoven and, with the help of the Cecilian, he played like him. As he went at this thing, his motions suggested revenge for those days when he was compelled to pump his father's organ till he collapsed. It seemed to me that he was now hell-bent on pumping this thing till it collapsed. It did! ◾

Wright's characteristic play with space is seen in the contrast between the expanse of the playroom and the narrow hallway that leads to it. Notice how the low, dark corridor ends in an explosion of space created by the high barrel-vaulted ceiling. Wright used this device in the Studio as well, where the intimately proportioned reception hall opens on to the dramatic, high-ceilinged drafting room. This westward-looking view of the room shows the restored balcony and the grand piano fitted into the wall. Normally, the balcony area is in darkness—giving the illusion that the room continues on and on, out of sight. On the railing stands a reproduction of the *Winged Victory* that had originally belonged to Wright's client William Martin.

The west façade of the Home hidden behind a screen of foliage, c. 1889–95. Photograph: The Frank Lloyd Wright Foundation, Scottsdale, Arizona.

LANDSCAPING

A building should appear to grow easily from its site and be shaped to harmonize with its surroundings if Nature is manifest there, and if not try to make it as quiet, substantial and organic as She would have been were the opportunity Hers.

—Frank Lloyd Wright
"In the Cause of Architecture," March 1908

IN HARMONY WITH NATURE

House Beautiful magazine in February 1897 noted about the Home: "It is so buried in trees and foliage that all its defects are softened and concealed. . . ." The untended lot appealed to Wright's ideal of Nature. His home, with its close-to-nature colors and materials, blended into the natural environment. This was a contrast to the other houses on Forest Avenue, which were set apart from the natural environment by their smooth clapboards and light colors.

Although the property was 88.3 feet wide and 165 feet deep, Wright placed the house close to the south lot line, leaving only enough space for a gravel drive between. This left the dense plantings intact, as a buffer, between the house and Chicago Avenue. The statement Wright was making with his house was about a person's place in the natural world, not about the owner's place in the manmade world. Throughout his career, harmony between landscape and architecture was central to Wright's sense of design. He termed the effect of synthesis among site, building materials, proportion, scale, interior space and ornament "organic architecture," akin to "a sense of completeness found in a tree or flower."

Exterior of the Home from the southwest. In the foreground is a white pine tree that was replaced by the restoration committee. Walkways were re-created according to historic photographs such as this one. 1889–95. Photograph: Avery Architectural and Fine Arts Library, Columbia University in the City of New York.

■ RE-CREATION OF THE HISTORIC LANDSCAPING

As much attention was paid to historical authenticity in restoring the landscaping as to the architecture itself. Landscape architects specializing in historic plant materials closely studied historic photographs to identify the plants seen in them. A ginkgo tree east of the Home plus a Kentucky coffee tree and a tulip tree in the Home's front yard all date from Wright's time. It would have taken the skills of a specialist such as landscape gardener John Blair to care for the coffee and tulip trees, as Chicago is at the northernmost boundary for their hardiness. Lloyd Wright recalled black and white walnut trees on the property, butternut trees along the south side of the Home, a honey locust near the front, a sugar maple in the front yard, the ginkgo tree that still stands and a black willow that was allowed to grow through the passageway between the Home and the Studio. Dense forsythia bushes bordered the lot at Forest Avenue, possibly placed there to create privacy. The restoration landscape architects situated a white pine in front of the south veranda to match historic photographs. They also re-created sidewalks and raised planting beds in accord with the photographic evidence.

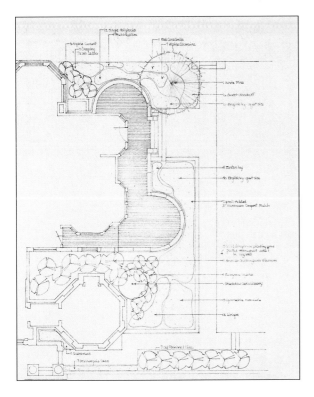

Landscape plan for the front yard, bordering Forest Avenue, 1986. Photograph: Frank Lloyd Wright Preservation Trust.

Although the front yard today is not as overgrown as historic photographs suggest, the Home is once more one with its site. The textures and colors of its natural materials—brick, cedar shingles and wood—are in perfect harmony with the natural landscape surrounding it. Photograph: Donald Kalec. Frank Lloyd Wright Preservation Trust.

A landscape plan was developed based on research about John Blair's garden, historic photographs, Lloyd Wright's recollections of a prairie garden on the site, and Maginel Wright Barney's description of the yard in her book *Valley of the God-Almighty Joneses.* In 1986 new sidewalks were poured, and prairie grasses, daylilies, sweet woodruff, ivy, wild ginger, Japanese lilac, hydrangea and lilies of the valley were planted. In the shade of the large ginkgo tree a garden of hostas, ferns and bleeding hearts was started. Along the eastern boundary of the lot, volunteers created a cutting garden. Fresh as well as dried cuttings from this garden are used in various rooms of the Home and Studio to replicate plant decorations seen in historic photographs.

Frank Lloyd Wright. Oak Park Studio (Oak Park, Illinois, 1898). From the series Ausgeführte Bauten und Entwürfe von Frank Lloyd Wright, June 1910. Berlin: Ernst Wasmuth. Photograph: Philip Mrozinski. Frank Lloyd Wright Preservation Trust.

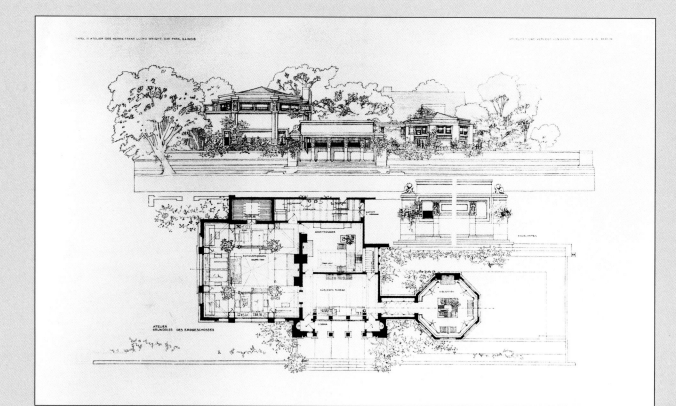

*T*he practice of architecture as a profession has fine art as well as commercial elements. . . . To develop in a better sense, this fine art side in combination with its commercial condition, the architect should place himself in an environment that conspires to develop the best there is in him. . . . in the hope of reaching these better results, a complete architectural work-shop has been constructed in Oak Park.

—From Frank Lloyd Wright's announcement on the opening of his Oak Park studio, 1898

Frank Lloyd Wright's Oak Park Studio is widely regarded today as one of the great spaces in American architecture. In this Studio between 1898 and 1909, Wright, working with other men and women who later became famous themselves, developed the Prairie style and changed American architecture.

Wright made numerous alterations to his work environment as his architectural vision developed. Charles E. White, one of the draftsmen in the Studio, wrote in November 1903, to his friend Walter Willcox, "[Wright] is certainly the most impractical man—is way behind in his work, but calmly takes seven weeks to alter his office." In another letter (May 1904), he stated, "Twice a year Mr. W. rearranges and changes the different rooms. He says he has gotten more education in experimenting on his own premises, than in any other way."

For his drafting room, Wright designed a 28-foot-square base topped with an octagonal drum. The balconied room rose to a peaked, beamed ceiling 23 feet above the floor. Lit by high, encircling windows, it was an inspiring workplace that contained a fireplace, decorative sculpture pieces and jars of wild flowers. A low, rectangular reception hall connected to the drafting room at one end, and to the other side of the office and an octagonal library at the other end. This binuclear plan, a central entry leading to areas on both sides, was a device Wright would use later in many of his public buildings.

The restoration of the Studio to its 1909 appearance required major reconstruction. Between 1982 and 1987, the process went forward in four phases. The structural stabilization, including excavation for a basement and full foundation rebuilding, came first. Exterior surface repairs and changes that included the roof, walls, windows, and decorative features followed. This phase also included the removal of the 1911 bedrooms over the drafting room and the reconstruction of the drafting room balcony. Then the interior was restored, including the magnesite (a historic composite flooring material) floor, art-glass windows and wood trim. The implementation of a furnishings plan continues to the present. Original pieces are added whenever possible; reproductions are made when the original furnishings are not available.

tural figures. A dramatic cantilevered overhang, considered a characteristic feature of his later work, covered the former Studio entrance (then a private porch) and projected over the public sidewalk. Restoring the building to its 1909 appearance necessitated difficult decisions by the restoration committee involving the removal of certain Wright-designed elements (such as the overhang) in the interest of historical accuracy.

Between 1925, when Wright sold the property, and 1974, when plans for restoration began, the Studio underwent even more changes. At one time it contained a group of rental apartments. Some original furnishings disappeared during this period, and the building itself deteriorated substantially. In 1956 Wright made additional alterations to the Studio for Clyde and Charlotte Nooker, who had purchased the Home and Studio in 1946. (They opened part of it for tours in 1965.) This complicated building history made the restoration of the Studio very extensive in terms of time, labor and financial resources. A $1 million fundraising campaign begun in 1981 resulted in support from many generous contributors, including the National Trust for Historic Preservation, Steelcase, Inc. (the project's major donor), American Express and United Technologies. The Foundation's commitment to the highest standards in restoration methods resulted in a cost of approximately $1.25 million by the time the Studio restoration was completed in 1986.

■ STUDIO BEFORE RESTORATION

In 1974, before restoration began, Frank Lloyd Wright's Studio was an amalgam of alterations made by Wright himself in 1911, 1925 and again in 1956. For the most part it looked as it did in 1911 when Wright remodeled his former studio into a dwelling for Catherine and the four children still at home. The two-story drafting room was made into separate floors: living spaces on the first floor and five bedrooms on the second floor. The upper level of the drafting room (seen above, on the left), originally an octagon, had been filled out at the corners to make a square that matched the original square base below. Up at the roofline, Wright had added decorative sculp-

Prior to the restoration, the Foundation used this bird's-eye view drawing of the Home and Studio as it looked in 1909 to illustrate the siting of the buildings on the lot, the relationship among the main parts of the buildings, and the interplay of geometric shapes.

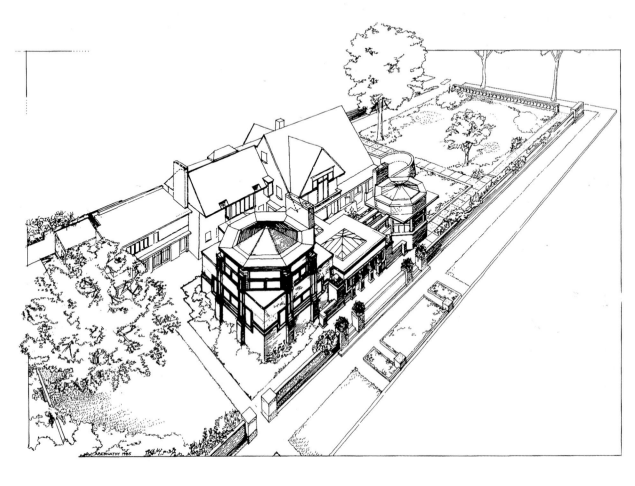

A bird's-eye view of the Home and Studio as the complex was supposed to look after restoration,1985. Drawing: Ann Abernathy. Frank Lloyd Wright Preservation Trust.

STUDIO CONSTRUCTION

Originally built on a very low budget, the Studio addition was basically standard wood-stud, brick veneer construction. Continuous common-brick foundation walls supported the outer edges of the drafting room, reception hall, and office. Wood girders and floor joists spanned brick piers to support the center sections of the building. The octagonal library was supported on eight brick piers. There was no basement under the Studio, so the floor joists were just above the ground, which brought the level of the main floor as close to grade level as was possible in frame construction. The exterior of common brick and cedar shingles matched the Studio to the earlier Home. ■

STRUCTURAL STABILIZATION

A major phase of the Studio restoration involved stabilizing the building both to stop its deterioration and to prevent any further settling, especially in anticipation of future heavy tourist traffic. The foundation of the Studio consisted originally of brick walls and brick piers spanned by wood beams just above grade. To temporarily replace this foundation, which was sinking unevenly, steel cylinders, or caissons, 30 inches in diameter and 12 feet long, were driven into the ground and filled with concrete. The photograph shows these caissons being installed to await the concrete. Located outside the building line, they provided temporary support for the east and north walls of the Studio while new concrete foundation walls were formed and cast directly below the existing upper walls. The new walls could support ten times the original load and formed a new basement as well.

In the photograph on the right, one of two new 27-foot-long steel support beams is being threaded under the drafting room from its east caisson to the chimney mass on the west wall. Two shorter beams were inserted from the north and supported on their northern ends by two more caissons beyond the building line. The long steel beams slid under the drafting room floor on portable rollers. These steel beams and columns that support the floor of the drafting room are visible today in the basement Research Center. During the restoration, a steel beam addressed to "Frank Lloyd Wright, Forest & Chicago, Oak Park" was found buried near the ginkgo

Installation of one of the caissons (concrete-filled steel cylinders) that temporarily supported the Studio walls while new foundation walls were built, 1983. Photograph: Frank Lloyd Wright Preservation Trust.

Steel beams were slid under the drafting room to support its floor, 1983. Photograph: Frank Lloyd Wright Preservation Trust.

tree just east of the Studio. Wright had used two steel beams in his 1911 remodeling to support his new second floor in the drafting room. The buried beam was presumably an extra.

The building needed to be made level; some floors had settled up to 3 inches from their original positions. A series of Y-shaped, temporary steel-channel trusses were bolted to each stud on the north and east sides of the drafting room to stabilize the building while it was being made level. Each truss brought the load down to the jack points on top of the caissons. The workmen in the photograph below are regulating the screw jacks under each truss as a part of the leveling procedure. Because the chimney mass on the west of the drafting room was stable, it served as the reference point for the leveling.

The excavation of a full basement provided some dramatic moments for visitors and volunteers as a tractor tunneled its way under the Studio, 1983. Photograph: Frank Lloyd Wright Preservation Trust.

The Studio had to be made level as many floors inside had settled and were no longer in their original positions, 1983. Photograph: Frank Lloyd Wright Preservation Trust.

■ BASEMENT EXCAVATION

On the recommendation of the restoration committee, the board of directors made funds available for excavating a full-depth basement rather than the originally planned crawl space under the drafting room, office and reception hall of the Studio. This new basement space provided easier access to the pipes, ducts and electrical conduit under the floor as well as much-needed room for storage and work space. Since 1987, it has housed the Research Center. The excavation of this space under the Studio was one of the most exciting and memorable events during the restoration. For two weeks a Caterpillar tractor dug under the building, which was dramatically held up only by temporary posts and the caissons. "Don't bump the pinheads!" was the exhortation to the tractor operator as he maneuvered between the precarious-looking supports. Tours operated throughout the restoration period, but access to the Studio rooms was not always possible.

For an entire winter, the Studio was encased in protective plastic while the roof was replaced, 1984. Photograph: Frank Lloyd Wright Preservation Trust.

The peaked crown of the drafting room roof was shingled as Wright had done. Tarred-felt roofing on the rest of the roof was replaced by single-ply membrane roofing during the restoration, 1984. Photograph: Frank Lloyd Wright Preservation Trust.

The building was stained its historic medium-brown color, 1984. Photograph: Frank Lloyd Wright Preservation Trust.

■ STUDIO EXTERIOR

Beginning in the fall of 1984 and continuing through that winter, the Studio was encased in a cocoon of plastic sheeting to protect exposed areas of the roof from the winter weather. A single-ply rubber membrane roofing was installed on almost all the flat roofs of the Studio in place of the original tarred-felt roofing. While this was a variation from the original material, its advantages of watertightness, ease of maintenance and durability outweighed exact historical accuracy—especially as most of the roof cannot be seen, except from the Home's second-floor windows. In the few places where Wright used tin sheet-metal roofing, as on the triangular corners of the drafting room, lead-coated copper (with the same appearance but much more durable) was substituted.

The peak of the octagonal roof over the drafting room was the only visible roof on the Studio, since the others were almost flat; Wright shingled just that small peak to match the roof of the Home. The rest of the drafting room roof was tarred felt. This peaked crown of shingles was carefully reproduced as Wright had built it. (The original shingled peak, much deteriorated, was found under several tarred-felt roofs.)

The red-cedar shingles and the redwood trim as well as board-and-batten sheathing on the Studio exterior were stained to appear as they did in 1909. Wright had even stained the bricks—probably to match the tone of the shingles and to protect the soft, absorbent brick from moisture. The appropriate medium-brown stain for the restoration was found on shingles under the brick firewall that was built in 1911 to separate the Home and Studio.

Chicago Avenue entrance to the Studio, c. 1898. Photograph: House Beautiful, December 1899.

STUDIO ENTRANCE

■ STUDIO ENTRANCE, 1898

The details marking the entrance to Wright's Studio announced to the world that this was no common workplace. This c. 1898 photograph of the Chicago Avenue entrance shows the loggia sheltering two hidden entrance doors. Richard Bock, a sculptor who was Wright's friend and who collaborated with him on commissions such as the Larkin Building (Buffalo, New York, 1906, demolished 1950), the Susan Dana House (Springfield, Illinois, 1902) and Midway Gardens (Chicago, 1913, demolished 1929) sculpted the two plaster figures, the Boulders, which were painted to resemble red granite and but-

tressed the ends of the upper entry wall. Bock was also the sculptor of the plaster stork capitals that decorated the loggia pillars. The sculptural decoration on these panels broke away from the classic tradition to represent a new American symbolism, one that was personal for Wright. A carved limestone plaque on the left of the entrance announced "Frank Lloyd Wright, Architect." Round limestone urns, a common feature of Wright-designed buildings, sat on square brick piers bordering the broad entrance steps. In 1905 these urns were moved to the entrance of the Home, where they remain today.

Chicago Avenue entrance, c. 1906.
Photograph: Frank Lloyd Wright:
Ausgeführte Bauten, *1911.*

■ 1905 ALTERATIONS

By 1905, Wright had added a second window band above the existing high windows in the drafting room and octagonal library to provide more light. By 1909, the upper band of library windows had been shingled over and a skylight added. The original entrance to the Studio featured broad steps leading from the street to the columned loggia. In 1905 a low brick wall, with two narrower entrances at each end, was built on top of the steps to discourage curious passersby. The new entrances in the wall were each flanked by square brick piers supporting half-spherical limestone urns for plants. These urns were larger than those they replaced, and they represented a three-dimensional version of Wright's logo mark of a cross within a circle within a square.

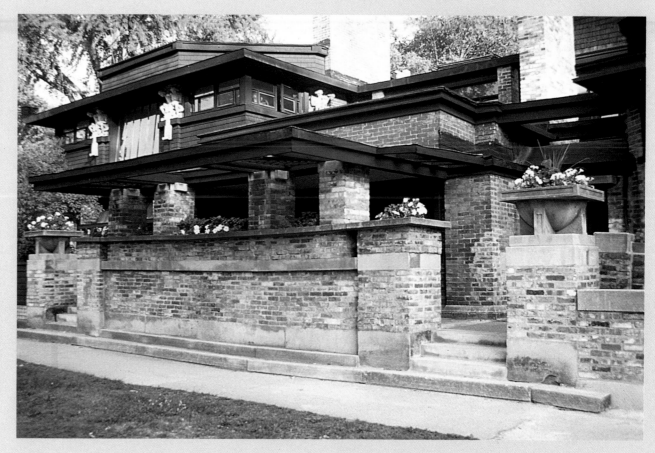

The removal of this 1911 cantilevered roof at the Chicago Avenue entrance generated a debate, 1975. Photograph: Frank Lloyd Wright Preservation Trust.

THE CANTILEVER CONTROVERSY

As part of the 1911 remodeling, Wright designed a cantilevered roof to shelter the former Studio entrance, which was then closed off from the sidewalk and used as a private porch by his family. During the restoration, this feature generated significant debate. Lloyd Wright, especially, argued against its removal. He considered the overhang Wright's final gesture to Oak Park. To him, the fact that it had not formed part of the building until 1911 was inconsequential. It was the spirit of the addition that mattered. But the restoration committee's decision to adhere to the target date of 1909 prevailed and was supported by Wright scholars and restoration architects who had reviewed the master plan in 1977. The cantilever was eventually taken down, along with other structural elements, such as the sculpted figures on the north and east façades, that dated after the 1909 restoration date. ■

■ DURING RESTORATION

The Bock stork capitals comprised a tree of life at the top, an open book of knowledge (or book of architectural specifications) below the tree and an architectural plan on a scroll in the center flanked by storks representing wisdom. Of the thirty-two plaster stork panels, nineteen were damaged and had to be replaced with reproductions made from one of the best-preserved originals. Each loggia pillar consisted of four stork panels installed to form a square capital. In the photograph, one of the panels is being prepared for installation. Most of the panels on the inner four columns, not exposed to the weather, were left in place and conserved. Reproduction panels were installed on the outer four columns, and the originals were saved in storage.

An artist from a local painting contractor applied the finish to all the stork capitals. She used two oil-based stains—a bronze brown and an olive green—applying each color separately with an airbrush to blend the colors. As the result of her work, the stork panels look as if they were made of bronze. Wright probably had the panels cast in plaster because he could not afford the more costly bronze.

The Boulder sculptures represented "the struggle of the oppressed and shackled soul to break its bonds and find self-expression," according to architect Robert Spencer in the June 1900 issue of *Architectural Review*. Richard Bock, their sculptor, had described them as "old and strong,

Sculptor Erin McNamara re-created a clay model of the Boulders from historic photographs, 1986–87. Photograph: Frank Lloyd Wright Preservation Trust.

A stonecutter made a replica of Wright's original name plaque to be installed in the wall at the Studio entrance, 1985. Photograph: Frank Lloyd Wright Preservation Trust.

depressed and dreaming of an epoch past and gone." The original Boulder sculptures were long gone. Cast of plaster from a clay original, they would have been vulnerable to the weather. To produce replicas, a sculptor worked from a historic line drawing and six historic photographs to sculpt a clay model. She also employed a live model who had to be tied up so that he could hold the contorted pose portrayed in the originals. From the clay model a three-part mold was created to cast lightweight concrete reproduction figures. The reproductions were painted to look like the simulated red-granite originals. Avoiding symmetry and to give the impression that each figure was different, Wright simply mounted them on the Studio facing in different directions. Sculpting two different figures would have been almost twice as expensive!

In 1911 Wright took the original limestone plaque that bore his name and logo (the cross within a circle within a square) to put into an entrance wall at Taliesin, his new home near Spring Green, Wisconsin. The restoration architects made a rubbing of the original and produced a drawing that guided the stonecutter in carving the reproduction seen in this photograph. American Express financed the reproduction.

The Chicago Avenue entrance restored to its 1909 appearance, 1999.
Photograph: Roger Straus III, Roger and Doris Straus Photography.

■ RESTORED STUDIO ENTRANCE

Alfred Granger wrote in "An Architect's Studio," published in *House Beautiful*
(1899), "Nothing could be more beautiful than the entrance to the Studio
from Chicago Avenue. Its proportions are so wholly satisfying as to repay the
closest study, while the detail is an integral part of the building and not an
applied decoration." The harmony of textures of natural materials—rough,
warm-hued Chicago common brick, limestone, sculptured granite and "faux"
bronze—adds to the richness of detail.

RECEPTION HALL

■ HISTORIC RECEPTION HALL

Upon entering the Studio from Chicago Avenue, Wright's clients found themselves in a low-ceilinged rectangular reception hall flanked by rooms with higher ceilings. In moving from the intimate reception hall to the higher-ceilinged drafting room or octagonal library, those spaces seem even more dramatic than they would have otherwise. Wright had used this spatial sequence in the playroom addition to the Home and later repeated it in other buildings, such as Unity Temple (Oak Park, Illinois, 1908).

In about 1905, Wright made changes to the reception hall. Angled side walls and a built-in secretary's desk were removed to make a larger rectangular room. Glazed doors were installed between the reception hall and drafting room. A weather skylight was added on the roof to allow natural light to filter through three long, narrow laylights of green and gold glass that ran the length of the room between deep beams in the ceiling. The original built-in desk and barrier (in front of the back wall) were replaced with a new plan desk under the art-glass windows facing the street. Contractors used the long plan desk as a place to unroll and check blueprints with Wright's draftspeople so the drafting room would not be disturbed. At the same time, the windows were redesigned and moved from the outside to the inside of the stork piers, becoming more of a light screen than windows in a wall. The Wright-designed spindle-backed chairs shown in the photograph were used by waiting clients or contractors.

Studio reception hall, facing east, prior to restoration, 1975. Photograph: Frank Lloyd Wright Preservation Trust.

Reinstallation of the reception hall laylights in 1985. Photograph: Frank Lloyd Wright Preservation Trust.

■ BEFORE AND DURING RESTORATION

This 1975 photograph of the Studio reception hall prior to restoration shows the original laylights and screen of windows still in place. The original stork capitals can be seen through the glass. A radiator cabinet with wood spindles (from the 1911 remodeling) is where the plan desk once stood.

The art-glass reception hall laylights and windows were in their original location when the Foundation bought the property in 1974. However, the skylight above them had leaked, causing the wooden beams, between which the glass panels were installed, to buckle. The buckled beams, in turn, put pressure on the panels, bending them. Fortunately, most of the damage was reversible. The bowed art-glass panels were gently flattened by the glass artist with the help of a truly low-tech method: weighing them down with up to five pounds of cat litter in plastic bags. Many solder joints were broken due to the initial bowing and subsequent flattening and needed resoldering. When the laylight panels were returned to their original positions in 1985, forty pounds of steel stiffeners were installed above the panels to keep them from deflecting in the future.

RESTORED RECEPTION HALL

This view of the reception hall shows it restored to its 1909 appearance. The metallic gold walls evoke an oriental effect and change color in the various lights of dawn to dusk and summer to spring. The laylights have been returned to the ceiling, the radiators are covered with stained basswood panels, a reproduction magnesite floor is in place and the restored stork capitals on the loggia columns are visible outside the art-glass light screen. In the background, the storage cupboards in the short hallway to the octagonal library can be seen. These cabinets were used by Wright to store samples of brick, wood and other architectural materials to show his clients. The chairs and plan desk are replicas based on historic photographs and originals owned by other museums.

OCTAGONAL LIBRARY

■ OCTAGONAL LIBRARY, 1905–1908

The octagonal library, shown here as it looked in about 1906, was used by Wright as an office and for consultations with his clients. High diamond-pane windows lighted the space and provided vistas of treetops. A second band of windows was added c. 1905, probably to match a similar change in the drafting room. In the octagonal library, the light from this new ring of windows was diffused by decorative wood-slat grille screens suspended from the ceiling. This band of windows was covered over on the outside by 1907.

Originally, the peaked plaster ceiling followed the underside of the octagonal pitched roof. By 1909 Wright had added a weather skylight over the center portion of the octagonal library. Light from the skylight was filtered through frosted glass arranged in a geometric pattern in a flat suspended ceiling. By 1905 a new set of bookcases (two with art-glass doors) and storage cabinets replaced the original bookcases on seven sides of the octagonal room. Wright also added swinging wooden frames, hinged to the cabinet posts, to display presentation drawings of his projects. Lights with conical green-glass shades were suspended from the ceiling. The Wright-designed print table shown in the photograph served as a space for laying out drawings. The chairs with square-spindled sides and backs were also designed by Wright. In 1907–08 Wright added a common-brick fireplace to the south wall.

Octagonal library, prerestoration, 1975. Photograph: Frank Lloyd Wright Preservation Trust.

■ BEFORE RESTORATION

This 1975 view shows the octagonal library interior prior to restoration. Although the room retained its distinctive shape and high clerestory windows, this image shows some of the changes Frank Lloyd Wright made in 1956 when the room was probably a bedroom for the Nooker family. The built-in dressing table, closet and Philippine mahogany woodwork seen here were probably added at that time. In the space between the octagonal library and reception hall was a bathroom. The carpet concealed a wood floor laid over the original magnesite flooring. To gain more wall space, the fireplace was covered over with lath and plaster.

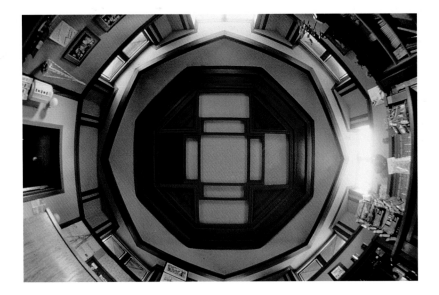

View of the octagonal library ceiling before restoration,
1975. Photograph: Frank Lloyd Wright Preservation Trust.

The octagonal library received a new foundation at the same time as the rest
of the Studio, 1983. Photograph: Frank Lloyd Wright Preservation Trust.

■ DURING RESTORATION

Before the restoration investigations began, the restoration architects thought the room had a paneled plaster ceiling. Further investigation revealed that what looked like plaster panels were really frosted glass panes that had been painted yellow, like the walls, when the weather skylight above had been roofed over. The entire ceiling structure, with its wood screen of overlapping squares and octagons, was intact and needed only refinishing.

The library's original foundation consisted of 18-inch-square brick piers at each of the eight corners, spanned by concrete beams at ground level (probably added by Wright in 1911 or 1925 to replace the original wood beams). Over time the brick piers had deteriorated and settled unevenly. To preserve the original octagonal building above, a continuous concrete foundation wall was formed below.

Steel bands around the library stabilized the structure while it was made level and a new foundation was poured, 1983. Photograph: Frank Lloyd Wright Preservation Trust.

Octagonal library interior during restoration, 1985. Photograph: Frank Lloyd Wright Preservation Trust.

To support the library while new foundation walls were being constructed directly below, two steel-pipe columns were inserted on each facet to support the existing concrete grade beam. Screw jacks on top of the columns allowed for leveling. The steel pipes were covered with a waterproof coating, and then the new concrete foundation was simply poured around these pipes. Above the steel pipes, temporary steel bands around the library base stabilized it while it was being leveled.

During restoration, the interior of the octagonal library was documented and then stripped of Wright's 1956 changes. A post-1909 window opening on a 1911 walled garden west of the building was also removed. The pho-

tograph shows the room awaiting the installation of the basswood trim and new windows. A fireplace had been covered up either before or during the 1956 renovation by Wright. Its Chicago common-brick construction, matching the material of the pre-1911 drafting room fireplace, suggested it was built no later than 1909, but its chimney did not appear in photographs until 1911. Faced with conflicting evidence about its date, the restoration architects left the fireplace in place, replacing its broken limestone lintel. This decision is in line with preservation policy. In the absence of any evidence, it is preferable to leave features in place than to guess at a date that affects their removal.

Restored interior of the octagonal library, 1999. Photograph: Tim Long. Frank Lloyd Wright Preservation Trust.

■ RESTORED OCTAGONAL LIBRARY

By mid-1984 the room looked once more like the 1909 octagonal library that Wright used as an office and for client presentations. Wright's use of geometry as decorative art is evidenced by the newly installed basswood trim that rings the room with a series of octagons at different levels. Each level rotates 22.5 degrees so that octagonal corners line up over the center lines of octagonal sides below, giving the room a spiraling quality. The high windows frame views of sky and trees that change with the seasons. Wright positioned them high on the metallic gold walls so his clients would not be distracted by the sights and sounds of Chicago Avenue. The lower west windows (which once opened on the 1911 walled garden) once again are bookcase doors. Only one of the cabinets that earlier lined seven of the walls remained at the time restoration began. The other cabinets were rebuilt following the example of the original. The table is believed to have been designed by Wright; it was found in the basement of the Home. The square-spindled chairs are reproductions of ones Wright designed for a number of other buildings. The weed holder is a replica of one Wright designed and often used in this room.

Studio drafting room, looking east, c. 1898–1900. Photograph: The Frank Lloyd Wright Foundation, Scottsdale, Arizona.

DRAFTING ROOM

■ **VIEW EAST, 1898**

The Studio drafting room as it looked in 1898 had "the air of a charming living room with inspiration everywhere," according to a contemporary *House Beautiful* magazine article. Wright worked with his staff in this room to design more than two hundred plans during his Prairie period, 1898–1909. The drafting staff worked at Wright-designed drafting tables and stools surrounded by Japanese art, classical sculptures and literary sayings. The two-story space was capped by a pitched octagonal ceiling supported by eight large wood beams. The balcony was used for allied arts such as sculpture, photography, painting and art glass.

WRIGHT'S ASSOCIATES AT THE OAK PARK STUDIO

In the eleven years that Frank Lloyd Wright's architectural practice flourished in the Oak Park Studio, Wright accomplished a third of his life's work. Contributing to his success were talented architects, draftsmen and artists, many of whom both adopted and influenced the Prairie style of architecture and eventually developed their own architectural practices. They came to learn from and work with the Master—some for years, others for weeks, still others on a project basis. Some had no previous drafting experience and had to be trained. Others brought architectural degrees with them. Wright did not pay much, but he allowed them to accept independent commissions, and he offered an environment fertile in artistic and architectural ideas. Wright described his method of working with his "loyal assistants" in his 1908 essay "In the Cause of Architecture":

> I assign to each a project that has been carefully conceived in my own mind, which he accepts as a specific work. He follows its subsequent development through all its phases in drawing room and field, meeting with the client himself on occasion, gaining an all-round development impossible otherwise, and insuring an enthusiasm and a grasp of detail decidedly to the best interest of the client.

Among the architects and artists who worked with Wright were Marion Mahony, Walter Burley Griffin, William Drummond, Charles E. White, Francis Barry Byrne, George Grant Elmslie, Francis Sullivan, John S. Van Bergen, Andrew Willatzen, George Willis, Harry Robinson, Richard Bock, George Mann Niedecken, Orlando Giannini and Isabel Roberts.

These architects were mostly social and religious liberals who participated in the city's many arts organizations, engaged in spirited discussions on modern sculpture and painting, made trips to the Art Institute of Chicago, went on expeditions to collect interesting grasses and branches with which to decorate the Studio, and relaxed together by going up to the playroom to use Wright's mechanical piano player.

All this camaraderie was not always without conflict. At times there were bitter arguments about the contributions of different individuals. When the Oak Park Studio was closed in the fall of 1909, however, Wright's associates took their intellectual and artistic experiences with them to develop their own—often significant—careers. Architectural projects just beginning in the Studio at that time were turned over to Hermann von Holst, assisted by Marion Mahony. Projects near completion in the Studio were finished by John Van Bergen and Isabel Roberts, who then closed up the building—officially ending Wright's Prairie years. ∎

Studio drafting room, looking west, c. 1898–1909. Photograph: The Frank Lloyd Wright Foundation, Scottsdale, Arizona.

Studio drafting room with changes made in 1905, looking east, c. 1906–09. Photograph: Frank Lloyd Wright: Ausgeführte Bauten, 1911.

■ **VIEW WEST, 1898**

The fireplace, with its Sullivanesque arched opening, was the focus of the 1898 drafting room. The decorative plaster sections above the fireplace were extra casts from a frieze Wright designed for the Isidore Heller House (1896) in the Hyde Park neighborhood of Chicago and executed by the sculptor Richard Bock. It was the first of many collaborations between Wright and Bock. Wright's interest in Native American design and crafts is seen in the rugs on the floor and on one of Wright's early chairs. This photograph was used to reconstruct the fireplace front.

■ **1905 ALTERATIONS**

By 1905, the drafting room had been remodeled to add the floating ledges or deck suspended below the balcony soffit, bringing the room down to a more intimate scale. These shelves were used to display sculpture and architectural models. Four tall, freestanding wooden cabinets provided storage space and created private alcoves for the draftsmen. Built-in storage and radiator enclosures under the windows integrated the heating and windows into the room's architectural composition. The inscription, hand-printed and tacked to the balcony face, is one verse from *McAndrew's Hymn* by Rudyard Kipling.

The Wright family's living room on the first floor of the former drafting room, looking west, c. 1911–25. Photograph: Henry Fuermann. Frank Lloyd Wright Preservation Trust.

■ 1911 ALTERATIONS

In 1911 Wright remodeled the Studio drafting room into a living room for his family's apartment. The balcony opening was floored over to create four children's bedrooms above. The new construction was supported by two steel beams running across the room and resting on brick piers within the room. Both piers and steel beams were boxed in and plastered. The fireplace was clad in Roman brick, and its opening was changed from the large round arch to a lower rectangular opening more in scale with the now lower-ceilinged room. The square-spindled chairs originally had been used in the reception hall and octagonal library. The glazed doors between the former drafting room and the reception hall were removed, and a pantry was added to the left, providing a wall for the inglenook seat. The *Wheatfields* pastel, moved from the Home living room, hung on the pantry wall above the seat.

Living room of the first-floor Studio apartment at the time the Foundation bought the building, 1974. Photograph: Donald Kalec. Frank Lloyd Wright Preservation Trust.

Living room of the second-floor Studio apartment before restoration, 1982. Photograph: Donald Kalec. Frank Lloyd Wright Preservation Trust.

■ BEFORE RESTORATION, FIRST-FLOOR STUDIO APARTMENT

By World War II, each floor of the Studio contained a separate apartment. In the living room of the first-floor Studio apartment, all the architectural features of Wright's 1911 remodeling for his family were still in place in 1974—two deep plastered beam covers running across the room, the plastered brick pier on the left, the Roman brick Prairie-style fireplace and even the corner inglenook seat.

■ BEFORE RESTORATION, SECOND-FLOOR STUDIO APARTMENT

This photograph, taken around 1982, shows the living room of the second-floor apartment, where originally the Studio balcony had been. A large sloping window was added when the four children's bedrooms were remodeled into a living room of the then-separate second-floor apartment sometime between 1918 and 1925. The stripes on the floor mark the location and thickness of the balcony wall before the second-story opening was floored over in 1911.

121

Master bedroom of the second-floor Studio apartment prior to restoration, 1982. Photograph: Frank Lloyd Wright Preservation Trust.

The chain harness as it was discovered, still in tension, continuing to hold the top of the building together against the pressure of the eight roof beams thrusting outward, as it had been doing since 1898. 1977. Photograph: Frank Lloyd Wright Preservation Trust.

■ STUDIO APARTMENT MASTER BEDROOM

What had been Catherine Wright's bedroom in the 1911 Studio remodeling, and after 1911 the master bedroom of the second-floor Studio apartment, was located directly above Wright's 1909 office. Wright added a small fireplace for Catherine, its flue running into the chimney from the fireplace below. The door to the right opened onto a roof deck. This room had to be totally removed so that the office below could be restored to its original one-story appearance with a skylight.

■ DURING RESTORATION

In 1975 the restoration architects searched unsuccessfully for the "chain harness" that they had read about in an *Architectural Record* article (June 1900) about Wright's work. This harness originally held the top of the drafting room octagon together. Separate chains supported the balcony. Not realizing that the harness was assembled in an octagonal shape, the team did not find it and assumed it had been dismantled during the 1911 remodeling. In 1977, when exploring between the attic floorboards and the 1911 apartment ceiling for another reason, architects discovered parts of the chain harness.

Right after the discovery of the chain harness, the restoration architects cut a hole in the Studio apartment bedroom ceiling to allow visitors a glimpse of the chain mechanism, 1978. Photograph: Frank Lloyd Wright Preservation Trust.

I lived in the second-floor Studio apartment from 1975 to 1982, the period when we conducted most of our research, including archeological probes, on the Studio. We had looked for the chain harness before, but hadn't found it and assumed it had been taken apart. One day in 1977, while probing beneath the attic floorboards, I reached down and felt a big cast iron ball with three large, taut chains connected to it. It was incredible! I started pulling up floorboards and found the harness. I called Bill Dring and Don Kalec [architects on the restoration committee], who came racing over. We took up the floor, and by God, we had uncovered the chain harness! It was so much more wonderful than we had imagined because it was a geometrically perfect octagonal tension-ring.■

—John G. Thorpe AIA
Restoration committee chairman

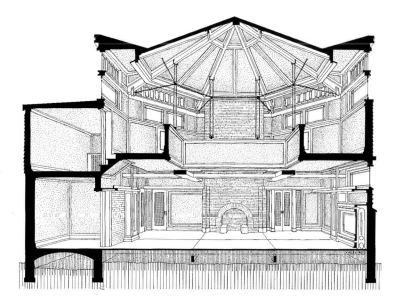

Cross section of the 1905 drafting room, showing the chain harness design. Drawing: Donald Kalec. Frank Lloyd Wright Preservation Trust.

■ CHAIN HARNESS RECONSTRUCTION

This 1983 cross-sectional drawing of the 1905 Studio drafting room shows clearly how the chain harness was integral to the room's structure. The horizontal chains of the harness formed an octagonal tension ring above the balcony opening—its eight corners connected with other chains to the eight corners of the drafting room. The harness resisted the outward thrust of the sloped roof, a task normally handled by horizontal joists. Another system of chains, not connected to the harness, consisted of eight doubled vertical chains (two on each balcony front) that suspended the balcony from the roof beams, thereby eliminating the need for supporting posts on the main floor. With his typical desire to express architectural structure, Wright left the chains exposed. The paired vertical chains, no longer needed when the balcony was floored over in 1911, were cut off and discarded. They had to be newly installed during the restoration.

■ DRAFTING ROOM FIREPLACE

Probes made before the restoration showed that the Studio's 1911 Roman-brick fireplace was a veneer, one brick thick, over the face of the 1898 Chicago common-brick fireplace. The 1911 Prairie-style fireplace was one of Wright's architectural features that some volunteers did not want to lose. However, once the drafting room was opened up into its 23-foot-high space, it was clear that the horizontally scaled fireplace was meant for a much lower ceiling. In Wright's 1909 vertically expansive drafting room, it would appear out of context. When the fireplace's Roman-brick veneer was removed, the stained common-brick fireplace with its Sullivanesque arched opening reappeared. Because of its condition, however, it was necessary to rebuild the fireplace. The wood seen in the fireplace opening was the centering (support) for the arch during the rebuilding. The carefully removed Roman brick, very difficult to find today, was used to rebuild a fireplace in another Frank Lloyd Wright home where the original fireplace had been removed.

Here, workmen are shown attaching the new vertical chains to the roof beams. Their ends will later couple to iron-ball anchors on top of the balcony railing. The original horizontal chain harness, exposed when the 1911 ceiling was removed, can be seen complete with its iron-ball connectors at the corners of the octagon. Today's building codes required the addition of steel beams in the balcony floor to give more support than Wright had provided with the suspension chains.

124

Studio drafting room during restoration showing construction of the balcony, 1984. Photograph: Frank Lloyd Wright Preservation Trust.

Staining of the drafting room ceiling beams during the restoration, 1985. Photograph: Frank Lloyd Wright Preservation Trust.

■ BALCONY RECONSTRUCTION AND SURFACE RESTORATION

The photograph on the left shows the framing of the new balcony floor around the 13-foot-square opening and two new steel I-beams concealed in the depth of the balcony floor framing.

During the restoration, the basswood trim in the Studio was carefully removed, and the wood, which had been "antiqued" with oil paint in the 1920s, was stripped by volunteers. The trim was stored for several years until the drafting room's replastering was completed, at which point it was reinstalled. As much of the original trim as possible was used, but some new basswood was required. The photograph on the right shows the drafting room ceiling beams being stained. All the wood in the Studio is basswood, stained to match an original piece of stained trim that had been covered over by the 1911 construction. During the stripping of the old basswood trim, four

shades (brown, white, red and yellow) were evident. In addition, there were pieces of new unstained basswood to consider. In order to achieve a consistent color on old and new wood, refinishing experts experimented until five different stain colors were chosen. By cutting the stain with alcohol and hand-rubbing each piece differently, a satisfactory match with the "control" trim was achieved.

The walls and ceiling in the Studio were originally surfaced with sand-finished plaster, applied over wood lath. Almost all the surfaces were in such poor condition because of water penetration and settlement that they had to be replastered. Samples of paint and plaster were taken from every surface, cataloged and put into the Research Center for future researchers. Walls and ceilings were covered with gypsum lath (today wood lath is used) and then plastered.

■ MAGNESITE FLOOR

When the Studio was built in 1898, it had dark-stained pine floors with areas of brown linoleum carefully laid, like the carpets in Wright's houses, in artful compositions, exposing the wood floors in certain areas, especially at the edges. By 1904 Wright had used a new composite flooring material in the Larkin Administration Building (Buffalo, New York, 1906, demolished 1950) called magnesite, which could be troweled over an existing wood floor no more than .5- to .75-inch thick. Wood chips (for texture) and different colorants (tan, brown and green being the most popular) could be added easily to the magnesium oxychloride cement base. Water was blended in to make a workable mixture. Wright covered all the floors in the Studio with this new flooring sometime around 1905, using a tan colorant and sawdust (hardwood and softwood) for visual texture. This durable and affordable material was typically used in high-traffic environments. The control sample was from the Studio balcony, covered in 1911 by another floor. It was used to determine the texture, thickness, color and composition of the reproduction magnesite. A contractor who had installed magnesite floors in the 1920s was hired to develop magnesite samples and train workers to install the now-historic material.

For the magnesite installation, the Studio drafting room floor was divided into nine sections (as it had been originally). Working three sections at a time, and starting with the perimeter of the room, a .75-inch-thick layer of magnesite was poured over metal lath stapled to the wood floor. The magnesite was leveled with a screed board, as the workman is shown doing in the photograph. Two to three hours later the surface was troweled and left to cure for a day. Then the form boards were removed, and work proceeded to the

A control sample of magnesite flooring and the ingredients (oxychloric cement and three grades of sawdust) that were used to match its composition for the restored magnesite floors in the Studio, 1986. Photograph: Frank Lloyd Wright Preservation Trust.

Installation of the Studio's magnesite floor during restoration, 1986. Photograph: Frank Lloyd Wright Preservation Trust.

neighboring sections. When the floor had completely cured, it was sanded and then sealed with tung oil. Once the floor had been used for a while, it took on the patina of well-worn leather, with color and tone variations, giving it a depth and beauty that Wright was seeking when he first began using magnesite. Examples of other buildings in which Wright also used magnesite are the Larkin Administration Building (Buffalo, New York, 1906, demolished 1950), Unity Temple (Oak Park, Illinois, 1908), the Meyer May House (Grand Rapids, Michigan, 1908) and the Frederick C. Robie House (Chicago, 1910).

■ DRAFTING FURNITURE REPRODUCTION

The drafting stools were modeled after those at Taliesin. At the time of the restoration, it was not known that one original drafting stool from the Oak Park Studio still existed. The original stool has a slightly slanted seat that enabled the architect to lean over the table to work. It was donated by a Wright family member to the Frank Lloyd Wright Preservation Trust's collections in 1993. No original Wright drafting table could be found, so reproduction tables were built by studying the size, scale and proportions of the tables in period photographs. Photographs of other architects' drafting rooms from Wright's time show that the draftsmen worked at drafting boards placed on top of sawhorses. Wright may have been the first to design a whole drafting table with a top that could be tilted by adjusting the location of pegs in the top's supports.

The stools and the bases for the reproduction drafting tables are made of oak finished with the same stain used on the rest of the oak in the Home. The drafting table tops are basswood, customary for drafting boards because of its fine grain and softness, which would accept thumbtacks easily (used by draftsmen for attaching drafting linen or paper to the table before drafting tape was invented).

Restored drafting room, view from balcony, 1986.
Photograph: Jon Miller, Hedrich Blessing Photographers.

Wright's concept of the drafting room as a great space with balconies flooded with light from high windows or skylights was a pattern he would use again in the Larkin Administration Building (Buffalo, New York, 1906, demolished 1950), Unity Temple (Oak Park, Illinois, 1908), S. C. Johnson Administration Building (Racine, Wisconsin, 1936) and the Guggenheim Museum (New York City, 1956). This view from the balcony shows how Wright employed engineering principles to produce a dramatically inspiring space. The horizontal chain harness keeps the beamed roof in place, while the doubled vertical chains suspend the balcony front from the beams. Wright's ingenious connection between the chain and the balcony is seen at the extreme left and right, where a wrought-iron yoke clasps a cast-iron sphere. It appears almost as visual poetry, not just a mechanical device. The tension stress is carried down to the balcony floor structure via a threaded rod inside the balcony railing; the iron sphere screws onto the end of the rod. While none of this remained after the 1911 remodeling, historic photographs and some physical evidence, such as rod holes found in the original balcony framing, enabled a re-creation. New steel beams in the balcony floor now provide added support to the balcony, as required by code, but the chains still carry part of the load.

Rudyard Kipling's lines from "McAndrews Hymn" (1893) were re-created and attached to the balcony railing, where they were in Wright's time. The deck is once again suspended over the drafting tables, and the cabinets are used for storing paper goods. The walls have been painted ochre-brown, their color in 1909.

The restored first floor of the drafting room contains a Wright-designed library table from the Francis Little Residence (Peoria, Illinois, 1902) holding a model of the Studio. This table is similar to one evidenced in Wright's plan of the drafting room, published in 1910. Also visible are the art-glass windows that existed in 1974, when the Foundation obtained the building. These mostly clear-glass windows, with a border delineated by strips of copper-plated zinc cames, were replacements for the leaded diamond-pane glass; between 1906 and 1908 Wright added them to most windows in the Studio. Reproduction drafting tables are arranged in pairs facing each other on three sides of the room, as they were depicted in Wright's plan of 1910. Tall paper-storage cabinets marked the corners of the central open space and created semiprivate alcoves for each pair of drafting tables. The prismatic Holophane glass globes provided general illumination. The green-glass shaded lights for drafting hung from the balcony soffit and could be adjusted up and down. (Both types of lampshades are currently manufactured by the Holophane company.) The cabinets below the windows conceal long hot-water radiators. As part of the Frank Lloyd Wright Preservation Trust's ongoing furnishings plan, selections of architectural models, sculpture, ceramics, artwork and period drafting tools continue to be added in order to suggest both the human occupancy of the drafting room and the architectural work accomplished here.

Studio drafting room, view west to fireplace wall, 1999.
Photograph: Tim Long. Frank Lloyd Wright Preservation Trust.

Streams of sunlight from the balcony windows show how natural illumination enters the drafting room from above. The large brick fireplace has limestone hobs that project out into the room—perhaps another Wright innovation. (Hobs had been used in colonial homes, but they were shelves within the fireplace to set pots for warming). In his studio, Wright used the hobs to hold firewood and as a place to sit. Artistically, the hobs make the fireplace more three dimensional.

The plaster panels on the brick chimney are new casts made from the originals on the Isidore Heller House (Chicago, 1896), designed just two years before the Studio. They will be lightly stained with the same brown stain Wright used over all the exposed interior brick. Wright frequently had extras made of his decorative designs and then used them for the enrichment of his own home and workplace. On the fireplace shoulder is a plaster cast of Michelangelo's *Head of a Slave.*

The Holophane prismatic globe lights are suspended by chains from the same cast-iron balls that connect to the balcony suspension chains—providing vertical vistas up the chains to the beamed ceiling above. The exposed cloth-covered electrical wiring and connections are early, rarely seen examples. Most of the electrical hardware was found in the building.

Although the room is rich in detail, the viewer's eye is attracted upward into the soaring space of Wright's 1909 atelier.

Studio office, facing northwest, c. 1898–1909. Photograph: House Beautiful, 1899.

STUDIO OFFICE

■ OFFICE, 1898–1909

This room, called a "study" on all of Wright's plans, seems to have functioned more as a general office for the architectural staff. The only telephone was here, and Isabel Roberts, the office secretary, must have done her typing at the long desk. The office opened directly to the drafting room and the reception hall. A skylight (with an art-glass laylight) was the principal source of illumination. Geometric art-glass windows behind the desk looked out onto greenery in the narrow space between the Home and the Studio.

This historic photograph shows the cubical chairs Wright created, one of his first designs for modern furniture. Inspiration was provided by the photographs and drawings on the high shelf; by nature, in the form of dried weeds (gathered from the fields just across Chicago Avenue) held in a

Wright-designed copper urn (left) and weed holder (right); by oriental art—a Japanese *kakemono* hanging on the wall; and by Renaissance sculpture—the plaster bas-relief reproduction of *Boys Singing from a Book,* purchased by Wright from P. P. Caproni and Brother, Boston. (The original marble panel, one of ten panels originally in the Cathedral of Santa Maria del Fiore in Florence, Italy, is by Luca della Robbia.)

Facing the desk, on the opposite wall, was a large round-arched fireplace made from Chicago common brick—a mate to the one in the drafting room that, in fact, shared a common flue. Wright liked to keep fires burning almost year-round for both cheer and atmosphere.

The grouping was similar to what Wright did the same year in the Home study. Notice how the transom went up into an open area at the edge of the ceiling, past the floorboards of the room above, into the high base of a closet on the second floor. From the dining room the transom windows just disappeared up out of sight, giving an intriguing lift to the room. Not seen in the photograph is a second transom above the first one.

As he had done in the drafting room, Wright changed the round-arch fireplace (not seen in the photograph) to one with a lower rectangular opening, in this case by completely rebuilding it with Roman brick. Only the hearth remained to furnish clues about the original fireplace.

■ 1911 REMODELING

In 1911, during the Studio's remodeling into living quarters for the Wright family, the former office was converted into their dining room. A bedroom for Catherine Wright was built directly above the roof of the office, which required the removal of the skylight (and a complete reworking of the ceiling trim). A walled garden was added to the west of the Studio to provide a private outdoor space for the Wrights. Access was through the art-glass doors seen here behind the dining table.

The whole 1911 ensemble of art-glass was complex. The paired doors and the sidelight were in an alcove, while their transom, which consisted of a pair of opening casements and a sidelight, was inset farther into the room.

■ BEFORE AND DURING RESTORATION

When the Foundation acquired the property, the paired art-glass casements in the transom were gone, replaced by a long clear-glass awning window. The transom sidelight can be seen here. The paired art-glass doors, sidelight, and the transom frame were carefully packed and stored before the Studio restoration. Since they were not part of the restoration period they were not

132

reinstalled, but they are a permanent part of the Foundation's collections and have been on display in several exhibitions.

In 1956 Frank Lloyd Wright was hired by then-owners Clyde and Charlotte Nooker to remodel—yet again—the former office/dining room into a dressing room, and the adjacent kitchen into bath facilities. This view (top right) shows the room as it was in 1974 after the Foundation took over the property. The Roman brick fireplace remained intact from the 1911 remodeling, as did most of the east end of the room. A shag carpet covered the painted magnesite floor. During the removal of a 1956 soffit, the 1909 ceiling trim pattern was revealed. This information, combined with knowledge of how Wright applied decorative trim in other buildings of the period, helped reconstruct the pattern on the office ceiling.

The room's original art-glass laylight had been removed in the 1911 remodeling. Re-creating the laylight was essential to restoring the 1909 office. A cartoon (paper pattern) was prepared based on historic photographs and used as a guide to compose the reproduction art-glass laylight.

Approximately 2,700 pieces of brilliantly colored glass made up the reproduction laylight. Having only black and white photographs to go by, the selection of colors was based on the closest example of Wright's art glass: the laylight in the reception hall. The cames also follow that example—brass-plated zinc, colonial style, which is very thin with a pointed profile.

1911 dining room (formerly Wright's office) art-glass doors that led to a private outdoor space, c. 1978. Photograph: Frank Lloyd Wright Preservation Trust.

Re-creation of the office art-glass laylight, 1986. Photograph: Frank Lloyd Wright Preservation Trust.

Assembly of the office art-glass laylight over a paper pattern, 1986. Photograph: Frank Lloyd Wright Preservation Trust.

Wright's office as the Nooker dressing room, looking north, prior to restoration, 1979. Photograph: Frank Lloyd Wright Preservation Trust.

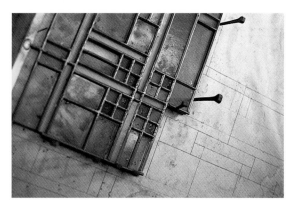

The Home and the Studio show an evolution of Wright's art-glass design over a twenty-year period as he perfected an abstract representation of nature that was a unique contribution to the decorative arts. The first pattern was a simple diamond pane made more sophisticated by a colored-glass border used in the Home (c. 1891) and the Studio (1898). Wright's next design was for the 1895 dining room addition—a copy of the lotus-based windows he had used on the second floor of the Winslow House (River Forest, Illinois, 1893), the first of his designs based on nature. Also from 1895 were the playroom bay windows with their abstract tulip design and the playroom bookcase doors with their geometric straight-line pattern of small squares surrounding a large clear center. By the time of the Studio reception hall and office laylights (c. 1905), the geometric patterns had become more complex. Wright pioneered such art-glass innovations as continuing a design from one window to the next or to a transom, using various widths of cames in the same window to make a more interesting design, and floating a decorative design in a window of clear glass.

Over the years, most of the art-glass panels in the Home and Studio had been reworked, and some were crudely held together with glue or structural adhesive. Many were replacement panels. Fortunately, enough original fabric existed so that, with the help of historic photographs, an art-glass expert could restore approximately half the number of panels and create ninety-four exactly sized reproductions. About 50 percent of the glass from existing windows could be reused; matches for the rest were obtained from stocks of antique glass.

The art-glass cames throughout the Home and Studio were originally of two materials: lead and zinc. The zinc cames had five different shapes in dozens of different sizes. Two of the styles were not commercially available at the time of the restoration, and expensive dies were made for those shapes. After the assembly, glazing, and soldering of the art glass, electroplating proved to be a challenge. The plating-bath solution available at the time was so corrosive that it dissolved the zinc. It also caused many difficulties in plating, rinsing and drying the panels. Eventually, the panels were rinsed in a custom-built rinse tank lined with polyethylene and filled with a neutralizing solution. Windows too large for the plating-bath container had to be made in sections and spliced together after being electroplated. A traditional recipe was used for puttying the glass: boiled linseed oil, turpentine, Portland cement and whiting. This mixture was poured over the panels, brushed between the cames and the glass, and left to dry. The art glass was then cleaned and polished before installation.

Wright's experiments with art-glass laylights and windows in the Home

RESTORED STUDIO OFFICE

The restored office shows the re-created laylight and west windows; the reproduction Wright-designed furniture of stained poplar, weed holder and urn; as well as a fragment from Wright's demolished 1895 Francis Apartments. The plaster cast of Luca della Robbia's *Boys Singing from a Book* was made by P. P. Caproni and Brother, as was the cast that Wright had, but it is not the same one. Decorative objects are displayed on the door-height shelf as Wright did when the space was an office. The wood trim on the walls and ceiling demonstrates how Wright used the linear quality of the wood

Reproduction office art-glass window being assembled, 1986. Photograph: Frank Lloyd Wright Preservation Trust.

Wright's office restored to its 1909 appearance, 1986. Photograph: Jon Miller, Hedrich Blessing Photographers.

and Studio matured into the "screens of light" of his Prairie residences. There, art-glass windows often wrap around the entire exterior of the house, bringing the natural world indoors, livening the light as it filters through the nature-inspired colors, providing privacy as well as variety to the dweller within.

To authentically re-create the 1909 building, all post-1909 art glass was removed, cataloged and preserved in storage. Every effort is made to make these pieces accessible to the public through periodic exhibits and loans to other museums, both nationally and internationally. ■

strips to enliven the space. Between the desk and the windows is a staircase leading to storage space and a toilet room in the basement for the draftsmen. The ochre-brown walls match the color of the drafting room. The office was restored with funds from Steelcase, Inc.

Passageway from the Home to the Studio, c. 1898–1910.
Photograph: The Frank Lloyd Wright Foundation, Scottsdale, Arizona.

There were no drawings of the passageway, so the photograph from the Taliesin archives was the only way we knew how to reconstruct it. Luckily, the photograph was taken looking in the direction of the stairs to the drafting room balcony. Even with the stairs in the photo, both John Vinci's office [restoration architect for the Studio]

PASSAGEWAY

■ PASSAGEWAY, 1898–1910

One of the trees on the wooded lot was a triple-trunk black willow growing east of the Home. When Wright decided to build the Studio, he chose not to cut down the tree but to incorporate two of its trunks into a passageway between the two buildings. This photograph, taken sometime between 1898 and 1910, is the only known photograph of the passageway from that time period. The pitched ceiling is quite low because the passageway had to fit under the rear overhang of the Home's second floor. Steps accommodated the change in level between the higher Home and the lower floor level of the Studio. The railings in the background were for the steps leading to a room above the drafting room's vault, and then on up to the balcony.

and I drew them several times over trying to make everything work out. Those stairs are very precisely done, and there are a lot of them in a very small space, to be able to get up as high as they do in a compact area. ■

—Donald Kalec
Director of Research and Restoration,
1981–86

Passageway from the Home to the Studio as a kitchen for the Studio apartment, c. 1911. Photograph: Henry Fuermann. The Frank Lloyd Wright Foundation, Scottsdale, Arizona.

■ 1911 REMODELING

In 1911, when Wright converted the Studio into living quarters for his family, the passageway between the Home and the Studio was sealed off from the Home by the brick firewall and became the kitchen area for the Studio dwelling. It was also expanded southward (to the left), filling in what had been an open area between the Home and the Studio. A skylight gave illumination, while a high window on the right (behind the plates) looked into the new family dining room (former office). The magnesite floor had been covered up to form a base for the cabinets. A drafting stool now did duty as a sink-side table. Just out of the photograph (to the left) would have been the icebox, "held in the branches of the willow tree," according to family members.

Installation of the 25-foot honey locust tree in the passageway so its branches threaded through the wall and ceiling, 1983. Photograph: Frank Lloyd Wright Preservation Trust.

Former passageway (facing south) remodeled as a dressing/bath area in 1956 by Wright for the Nookers, 1983. Photograph: Donald Kalec. Frank Lloyd Wright Preservation Trust.

■ DURING RESTORATION

In October 1983, when the passageway was being restored to its 1909 appearance, a young 25-foot honey locust was substituted for the long-gone willow. A replacement tree the same age as the mature willow would have been impossible to transplant. The locust was selected because, unlike a willow, it resists pollution and tolerates shade, can survive with little water, and is less likely to invade water pipes. Installing two trunks of the locust inside the passageway framework proved a challenge because the space did not permit the use of cranes or other power equipment. Twelve men worked three hours to install the tree. Within two years after the restoration, the two interior trunks died; the tree was too young to withstand having part of its trunk warm and part frozen in the winter. The outside trunk lived and continues to shade the passageway in the summer.

■ BEFORE RESTORATION

Wright remodeled the passage area for the Nookers in 1956 to serve as a kitchen and dressing room. The wall between the office and the passageway was removed, and clothes storage cabinets were added. The door to the right led to a shower, located exactly where the original passageway met the Home. The large mirror is in the expansion area created in 1911 when the passageway was made into the Wrights' apartment kitchen. Record drawings and photographs were made, and representative materials samples kept, of the 1956 Wright remodeling before the space was restored to its 1898 functions as a passageway and office.

The restored passageway between the Home and the Studio, 1986. Photograph: Jon Miller, Hedrich Blessing Photographers.

■ RESTORED PASSAGEWAY

Thanks to the details visible in the historic photograph, the restoration architects were able to re-create the passageway exactly as it appeared in 1909. The wood banding on the ceiling and the Studio balcony stairway's square wooden spindles attest to the oriental influence on Wright's designs. The window on the right looks out to a narrow space between the Home service wing and the Studio. The main trunk of the tree is just outside the glass. Wall-mounted light sconces are replicas of examples found in the Studio and are positioned as shown in the historic photograph. Carbon-filament lightbulbs glow softly, just as they did in 1909.

■ PANORAMA OF CHICAGO AVENUE FAÇADE AFTER RESTORATION

With the completion of the restoration, the clarity of Wright's geometric composition can be seen. Here, in his design for his own work space, Wright was able to distinguish the various functions of his studio, making each part a separate form—harmonious but different—in a 75-foot-long asymmetrical arrangement. The articulation of interior space and exterior form enabled the outside of the building to reveal what was happening inside. Limestone urns filled with plantings form two gateways to the entire composition. One of the urns was missing and had to be reproduced during the restoration. The parkway in front of the building was re-created according to historic photographs and drawings. The natural textures of cedar shingles, board-and-batten,

common brick and limestone marry the composition to its site, so that the building "grow[s] up out of conditions as a plant grows up out of soil, as free to be itself, to live its own life according to nature as is the tree." (*An Autobiography,* 1943)

Inside, Wright's remarkable workplace appeared once again as Alfred

Granger described in his 1899 article "An Architect's Studio" in *House Beautiful:* "Inspiration everywhere, the right sort of inspiration, which recognizes the wondrous beauty of the works of the past, while at the same time it lives in the world of today and cares for its simplest flowers."

CLIMATE-CONTROL SYSTEM

The Wrights' home was originally heated with gravity-fed hot air from a coal-fired furnace in the basement. This system was replaced by a hot-water heating system at a later date—certainly by 1901, when the Home and the Studio were connected to the Yaryan system that piped hot water from a central source throughout Oak Park. At this time, Wright added hot-water radiators in the Studio and in some rooms of the Home. In 1955–56, the Yaryan system was shut off, and the owners of the building added new boilers in the basement of the Home as well as in a dugout crawl space beneath the Studio.

In the 1970s, during restoration planning for the Home and Studio, the restoration committee decided to restore the building without a cooling system. It was believed that the interior finishes of a historic building would be compromised if new air-conditioning were introduced.

During the restoration of the Home, the existing hot-water radiator system was used to heat the building with the help of a small, newly installed forced-air system. Air conditioning was discussed, but the ducts in the walls were too small for the quantities of cool air that would be required, and the cost was prohibitive.

In 1987 a General Conservation Study of the collections determined that the collections needed museum standards of care and protection from deterioration in order to be preserved for future generations. The conservators recommended full climate control, with optimum humidity of 50 percent and temperature of 70°F for the objects in the collection.

However, the debate about caring for the collections at the expense of the building itself continued. House museum professionals differed on the subject, and the cost was still a major concern. In 1988 the Foundation hired an environmental conservation consultant to analyze the building and collections. The study of conditions in various rooms showed significant swings in both interior temperature and relative humidity levels within a single day, brought on by the heavy level of tourism in the hot summer months. The latent heat was negatively affecting the visitors as well as the collection. It was clear that without climate control, the life of the materials in the collection would be shortened. Moreover, funding for furniture conservation was difficult to procure because of concerns that the furniture would not be housed in a climate-controlled environment.

The study recommended "design parameters" (temperature and humidity levels) for nine climate-control zones. These parameters were to be changed gradually from summer to winter to minimize any shock to objects and to the building.

To design the actual climate-control system, heat/loss gain calculations were completed for each room, using "as-built" drawings and an insulation schedule. Operating cost projections were developed.

The mechanical system that was finally selected consisted of fan coil units for each space, with separate condensers outside the building. This system provides air to isolated spaces while minimizing the installation of ductwork.

It also allows for temperature and humidity controls in individual spaces. Each fan coil has a steam generator to control humidity on a zone-by-zone basis. Numerous exterior condensers are located in places where they are both efficient and out of sight: hidden in bushes, under porches and on rooftops.

Each room was dealt with separately when it came to deciding where to install the fan coil units and how to introduce air into the room. Priorities were to incise the original Wright-era fabric of the building as little as possible and to make the supply and return openings as invisible as possible. Of sixteen rooms, only one—the playroom—has grilles placed in original ceiling plaster. All the air openings, although unobtrusively incorporated into the interior finishes, distribute the air evenly.

A computerized control/sensor system monitors sixteen microclimates and automatically corrects for proper temperature and humidity. It adjusts to changes due to time of day, air pressure, sunlight patterns, doors opening, and groups of tourists entering and leaving the room. Sensors installed inside walls monitor the walls for potential moisture problems.

The installation of the climate-control system was made possible in part by grants from the National Endowment for the Arts, a federal agency, and from the National Trust for Historic Preservation. In-kind donations were received from Carrier Corporation–United Technologies, Dri-Steam Corporation, and Air Products Equipment Company. ■

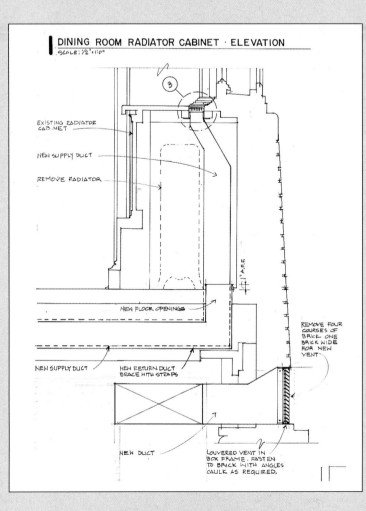

Dining room radiator cabinet section. For the dining room, fan coils are installed at the basement ceiling, with short ducts leading up to the dining room cabinets. The supply diffusers are in the tops of the cabinets, custom-fit to the original slot openings. The aerodynamic metal diffusers allow for efficient airflow and minimize damage (caused by airflow) to the wooden cabinets. Diffusers are wood-grained to blend with the adjoining oak. The return duct is installed inside the cabinet, with air flowing through the existing cabinetry base. Drawing: Karen A. Sweeney. Frank Lloyd Wright Preservation Trust.

143

Thanks to the elaborate care that has been orchestrated on its behalf, the Frank Lloyd Wright Home and Studio has survived the twentieth century, along with Wright's two later homes in Wisconsin and Arizona and his other extant architectural works. It is thus safe to assume that, with diligence, his heritage will remain intact. What remains unclear, however, are the revisions and modifications that will be made as future generations discover and reinterpret the structures, ideas and writings by Wright and about Wright. In this sense, even though the buildings remain intact, the debate about the ideas which drove the design will continue and the legacy will change as it is reviewed in the context of the social and political issues of the time.

The 1999 film by Ken Burns for public television about the life and work of Frank Lloyd Wright emitted the usual flurry of excitement and comment. A good historian, Burns used the Aristotelian three-act format: Wright was born, he lived, he died. For many viewers, the old iconoclastic image of Wright as a womanizer, deadbeat dad and debtor prevailed, but his vivid personality and strong philosophy were easier to accept in 1999 than they were at the end of the Prairie period, when he left his family and built his new home, Taliesin. In some measure, our revisionist view of this visionary may be attributed to a society that has become accustomed to showmen. Indeed, we all but demand them. The documentary may even have illuminated how this most extraordinary architectural talent of the twentieth century survived. The Burns film was great entertainment and a fair portrayal of this creative man. But, in a very important area, it failed. The present sank from sight, and we were left with a historical artifact. Where were the clients in this film? Where were those large, well-known corporations whose investment in Wright years ago has paid off many times over: Johnson Wax Company, Steelcase, Inc., the Solomon R. Guggenheim Foundation? Where was the pressing message that "design matters"?

In my view, this is the message that should resonate for architects and communities today. Because the film was bereft of current context, its ability to translate Wright's message seemed entirely lost. So where does Wright's message go? Is it to be left in limbo, or is it to flourish as a promoter of new spaces, new languages in action, new faces and aspirations? Design makes a difference. It projects life into the environment, into selected space, into beauty, into value. It shows how the analytical and creative mind can leap across the gaps that separate us from the past and the future. There are innumerable other examples of design which bring us into the present and move us into the future, a place where Wright's work always resided.

"My next building will be my best," my grandfather used to say. He understood that nothing stands still and that change is implicit in everything around us. He was a man who took the risk, commanded the courage, found the clients and led architecture through the jungle that was "tradition" to find new fields and forms. Countless others followed. European architects, especially, took up the challenge to explore design and new architectural forms.

Wright's legacy, as regards his buildings, is clearly recorded and protected by vast numbers of people and institutions the world over, including the owners of his some 330 surviving buildings, the Frank Lloyd Wright Preservation Trust, the Frank Lloyd Wright Building Conservancy, The Frank Lloyd Wright Foundation and the Taliesin Fellowship. His legacy is also protected by practicing architects everywhere who recognize the contributions of an architect who looked at the human condition and the environment and harnessed his talent to address the quality and design of life.

What is not protected is the message Wright sent that "design matters." Instead, we unfortunately witness environmental destruction, urban chaos, community deterioration and a growing body of nomads who change jobs and residences every five years. That Wright's Usonian housing and prefabrication systems failed to even dent the post-World War II surge of repetitious, badly planned housing developments is part of the failure of the twentieth century. Architects and planners share the responsibility for this impasse. With burgeoning global populations and rising expectations, the twenty-first century will have to address such issues boldly.

By way of a small introduction to this new century I recently attended a jazz concert in the Rotunda of the Guggenheim Museum in New York City. I had at long last set aside enough time to "think" my way through the building. Hundreds of visitors, young and old, moved down the long, coiling ramp studying the paintings and occasionally leaning over the railing to look down at those of us sitting below among the sculpture exhibits with our coffee and pastries. The music wafted upward through the great space to the skylight overhead and we applauded. Here then, was what Wright, the architect, wanted: To bring to this most densely populated city a secure and beautiful place where the interplay of natural light, art, and people in motion vibrated with delight and discovery. The present-day activity in the museum was a clear testament to his vision.

After the concert, I walked up the ramp to the Tower Room to see architect Frank Gehry's preliminary models and drawings for another Guggenheim Museum on the East River: A vast platform stretching out into the river, with exhibit cubes arranged both vertically and horizontally to form the core of the new space. Draped over the entire complex was Gehry's undulating, shimmering titanium robe. Was this new work—after the Guggenheim Museum in Bilbao, Spain—by architect Gehry an iconoclastic trademark, or was it the rendition of a new technology seeking its place and form in today's society? Perhaps the emergence of new architecture is the true legacy of Wright: The

knowledge that talent and courage can work its way through the system using energy and skills to produce a better, more interesting, more beautiful quality of life. The example of Wright, who focused his talent on bringing forward ideas for our delight and well-being, will be remembered as a major catalyst. The twentieth century has given us many fine, innovative and sensitive architects. Our current abundance of talent may well be another facet of Wright's legacy.

Today, as Fallingwater, in Bear Run, Pennsylvania (1940), and the Frederick C. Robie House in Chicago (1910), undergo restoration, we can begin to rethink historic preservation. Preservation should take us into a productive future rather than attempt to hold on to the past as a model for the present. The difficulty with historic preservation has always been that people reject the present in favor of the past while attempting to replicate the past in an effort to improve the quality of life. But, history does not repeat itself explicitly or willy-nilly. Historic preservation is an ongoing endeavor that needs the presence of new thinking and new directions. In our world of mass markets and global communication, growth of any kind has become a design issue. We need bold ideas and courage to make decisions that do not exclude anyone. Diversity, equality and justice are the benchmarks for everyone but those who use the past as a place to escape to. Today we recognize that there are new talents, new forms—in fact, a paradigm shift—in the way we have lived since Wright's death in 1959. Marveling at the past is not an idle pursuit. Preservation and conservation provide a much sought-after historic record for study. The past is a foundation for the future, enabling us to discover the fact and truth of those larger issues involving the planet and the universe. But if the past acts as an anchor, we lose. If it acts as a propeller, we win.

—Elizabeth Wright Ingraham, architect
Colorado Springs, Colorado, July 2000

RESTORATION CREDITS

Restoration and Preservation of the Frank Lloyd Wright Home and Studio, 1974–2000

Owner
National Trust for Historic Preservation

Restoration and Operation
Frank Lloyd Wright Preservation Trust (formerly known as Frank Lloyd Wright Home and Studio Foundation)

Architect of Record
The Restoration Committee of the Frank Lloyd Wright Home and Studio Foundation
John G. Thorpe AIA, William B. Dring AIA, Donald G. Kalec, Jack Lesniak AIA, Andrew Bober AIA—Chairpersons
Carl J. Hunter AIA, Karen A. Sweeney AIA—Vice Chairpersons
Donald G. Kalec, Karen A. Sweeney AIA—Staff Directors of Restoration
Ann K. Abernathy—Staff Project Architect

Special Restoration Consultants
Lloyd Wright, architect; David Wright; Eric Lloyd Wright, architect.

Associated Architects
The Office of John Vinci, Robert A. Bell Architects Ltd., Fred C. Burghardt AIA.

Engineers
Perkins and Will Engineers (structural); Bruno Blachowicz P.E. (mechanical); Steven Glenn, Energy Conscious Design Associates (mechanical); Gavlin and Reckers (structural); Eugene Dubin (structural).

Consulting Services
Robert A. Furhoff (paint analyses); Martha Scatterday (landscape design); Matthew Mosca, National Trust for Historic Preservation (paint analysis); Nathan Stolow FIIC, FAIC (climate control).

General Contractors
G. A. Johnson and Son, Evanston: Jack Galbraith—Vice President, Leonard Fieroh, Lawrence Balcer, Peter Korab—superintendents; Sumner Sollitt Construction Co., Chicago; Frank Stowell and Sons, Evanston; Don Taylor Builders, LaGrange.

Restoration Volunteer Crew Leaders
Donna J. Davis, Karen A. Sweeney, Cynthia Pry.

The Restoration Committee
Chairs, Senior Staff Architects and Crew Leaders, Michael Crist, Grant Dahlgreen, Gary Dawkins, Mark DeWalt, Judy Faulhaber, Frances Figg, William Furlong, John Hammond, Charles Herrig, Peter Korab, Ken Lee, William J. Mahalko, Joy Malnar, Bob Mifflin, Greg Mihalic, Mark Nichols, Bruce O'Brien, Georgia Rush, Christine Smolen, David Sokol, Elmer Stecher, Robert Stephens, Greg Tornatore, Richard Twiss, Wes Wieting, Mary Woolever.

Staff Architects and Draftspersons
Morgan Sweeney, William J. Mahalko, Maria T. Roche, Cynthia Muller, Herbert Hoppe, George Witascek, William Foelmer, Ann Williamson, Brian Pierce.

FRANK LLOYD WRIGHT HOME AND STUDIO FOUNDATION (1974–2000)

Executive Directors
Paula Nelson, Victoria Behm, Carla Lind, Elaine Freed, Sandra Wilcoxon, Natalie Hala, Joan B. Mercuri.

Board Presidents
Dawn Goshorn Schumann, William B. Dring, Carl J. Hunter, John G. Thorpe, Ann Y. Marohn, Carolyn Lang, Gloria Garofalo, Dr. Terry Light, Linda Hutchinson, James Yunker, Nancy DeSombre, Barbara Schnitzer, Robert Wetherald.

DECORATIVE ARTS CRAFTSPERSONS AND CONSULTANTS
(Cities for all businesses are located in Illinois unless specified otherwise.)

Art Glass
Cooper Art Glass, Ormond Beach, Florida
Wenz Art Glass, Grayslake
Jacqueline Wright, Colorado Springs, Colorado
Prism Art Glass, Oak Park
Charles Lotton, Lansing

Decorative Millwork and Reproduction Furniture
Interior Woodworking, New Paris, Indiana
Mark Duginske, Wausau, Wisconsin
Bradford Corporation, Bensenville
Elmer Stecher, Oak Park
Northwest Mill & Supply, Carpentersville
Hohmeier Lumber & Mill, Chicago

Decorative Plaster

C. G. Girolami Co., Chicago
Luczak Brothers, Chicago
Erin McNamara, Chicago

Decorative Stonework

Galloy and Van Etten, Chicago

Exterior Sculpture

Architectural Terra Cotta & Tile/Erin McNamara, Chicago

Mural Conservators

Faye Wrubel, Karen Knight, The Art Institute of Chicago
Anne Rosenthal, San Rafael, California
Peter Kulish, Chicago

Stencils

Chicago Architectural Arts Studio, Chicago
Robert Furhoff, Chicago

Consultants

Tim Lennon, Oak Park
Tim Samuelson, Chicago

MAJOR BUILDING TRADES AND SUPPLIERS

Cabinet & Trim Carpentry

Jeff Jeffers, New Lenox
G. A. Johnson & Son, Evanston
Sumner Sollitt Construction Co., Chicago
Don Taylor Builders, LaGrange
Steger Construction, River Grove
Elmer Stecher, Oak Park
Peter Korab, Oak Park
Gary Steiner, Oak Park
Hermann Wieland, Chicago

Climate Control

United Technologies–Carrier Corporation, Hartford, Connecticut
Dri-Steam Corporation, Hopkins, Minnesota
Air Products Equipment Co.
Commercial Heating and Cooling, Downers Grove

Concrete

G. A. Johnson & Son, Evanston
Robert Del Sarto Co., Berwyn
Daker Construction, Willowbrook

Demolition

Restoration Volunteer Crews
General contractors

Electrical

Midwest American Electrical, Oak Park
Fifth Avenue Electric, Oak Park
Marsala Engineering, Brookfield
Accord Electric, Oak Park

Floor Refinishing

A and K Floor Company, Oak Park
John Hammond, Elmhurst

Foundations

Dave Pate & Sons, Roselle

Insulation

Wilkin Insulation/Certain-Teed Corp., Chicago
Ruddy Insulation

Landscaping

The Natural Garden, St. Charles
T&Z Nursery, Winfield

Lighting Fixtures

Wilmer Snow & Co., Chicago
Holophane Division, Manville Corp.

Magnesite Flooring

Hascek-Melville Co., Maywood

Masonry

Mahler Construction Co., Barrington
Frank Smit, LaGrange Park
Robert Cox
DJ Building Maintenance, Franklin Park

Masonry Cleaning

Downstate Restoration, Chicago

Paint Materials

Benjamin Moore Paint Co., Melrose Park
J. C. Licht Company, Oak Park
Wallace Gilmour's, Oak Park

Painting and Staining, Exterior

J. Bernard Mullen Company, Oak Park
John Hammond, Elmhurst

Painting, Interior

Restoration Volunteer Crew

Plaster

Luczak Brothers, Chicago
William McNulty & Sons, Oak Park
John Hammond, Elmhurst
Eli Ponich

Plumbing

John R. Gilchrist & Sons, Oak Park
J. C. Geyer Plumbing, Oak Park
W. Gorin Smith, River Forest
Amcon Inc., Chicago

Plumbing Fixtures (Catering Kitchen)

Elkay Manufacturing Co., Oak Brook

Roofing

Mader Roofing, Oak Park
Marris Roofing Co., Hickory Hills
Hans Rosenow & Co., Chicago

Salvage Items (Hardware, Plumbing Fixtures and Fittings, Floor Registers)

Salvage One, Chicago
The Renovation Source, Chicago
Liz's Antique Warehouse, Chicago
John R. Gilchrist, Oak Park
Various national historic hardware sources

Security

Forest Security Systems, River Grove
SecurityLink from Ameritech, Oakbrook Terrace

Sheet Metal

Racine Sheet Metal, Chicago
Albany Sheet Metal, Chicago
Sytsma Sheet Metal, Bridgeview

Soil Testing

Soil Testing Services, Northbrook
Conrad DeLatour & Associates, Des Plaines

Special Castings and Metals

Spanjer Brothers, Chicago
Mueller Ornamental Iron, Chicago

Tile Setting

Tile and Carpet Center, Oak Park

Upholstery

Frank D. Ibach & Sons, Oak Park
Knoll International, New York City
Tailored Draperies, Oak Park

Wall Coverings

New York Central Supply, New York City
Kiesling Hess, Philadelphia, Pennsylvania
Orinoka Mills, Philadelphia, Pennsylvania
Sloan Davis, Oak Park

Woodwork Finishing & Staining

Johnson's Restoration Service, Oak Park
Woodwork Restoration, Inc./Pam & Phil Eberlin, Chicago Heights
John Hammond, Elmhurst

WITH APPRECIATION

All donors to the permanent collection
Avenue Bank, Oak Park
Business Interiors, Inc., Oak Brook
Forest Preserve District of DuPage County
Foundation members and other donors to the Restoration Program
Good Time Stove Co., Goshen, Massachusetts
John Tilton, River Forest
Michael O'Connor, Oak Park
Muse Piano Workshop, Oak Park
National Trust for Historic Preservation, Washington, D.C.
North Boulevard Antiques/John Toomey, Oak Park
Oak Park Conservatory
Oak Park Development Corporation
Residents of Oak Park and River Forest
Steelcase, Inc., Grand Rapids, Michigan
Village of Oak Park

REFERENCES

Abernathy, Ann. "Outline: Restoration Alternatives, Goals and Procedures." Unpublished Restoration Notes. Frank Lloyd Wright Home and Studio Foundation, 1985.

Abernathy, Ann and John G. Thorpe. *The Oak Park Home and Studio of Frank Lloyd Wright*. Oak Park, IL: The Frank Lloyd Wright Home and Studio Foundation, 1998.

Alofsin, Anthony, ed. *Frank Lloyd Wright: An Index to the Taliesin Correspondence*. Vol. 5. New York: Garland Publishing, Inc., 1988.

Baxter, Catherine Wright. Interviews by Donald Kalec, June 1975, November 1, 1975. Research Center of the Frank Lloyd Wright Preservation Trust.

Baxter, Catherine Wright. Letter to Donald Kalec, undated. Research Center of the Frank Lloyd Wright Preservation Trust.

Bellmore, Audra. "A 25-year Legacy." *Wright Angles* 25, no. 2 (May–July 1999):3–6.

Birk. Melanie. "Revisiting the Restoration: Part Two." *Wright Angles* 20, no. 3 (August 1994):3–7.

Birk, Melanie. *Frank Lloyd Wright and the Prairie*. Frank Lloyd Wright Home and Studio Foundation. New York: Universe Publishing, 1998.

Brenner, Douglas. "Wright at Home Again." *Architectural Record* (September 1986):118–125.

Dressel, Janet. "An Oral History Regarding the Frank Lloyd Wright Home and Studio Foundation." Interview by Zarine Weil, 1999. Research Center of the Frank Lloyd Wright Preservation Trust.

Dring, Bill. "An Oral History Regarding the Frank Lloyd Wright Home and Studio Foundation." Interview by Christopher Farmer, 1997. Research Center of the Frank Lloyd Wright Preservation Trust.

Duginske, Mark. "Restoring Wright's 1895 Skylight." *Highland Hardware* (1983):4–6.

Gill, Brendan. *Many Masks: A Life of Frank Lloyd Wright*. New York: G. P. Putnam's Sons, 1987.

Granger, Alfred H. "Successful Houses." *House Beautiful* I (February 1897):64–69.

Granger, Alfred H. "An Architect's Studio." *House Beautiful* VII (December 1899):36–45.

Harrington, Elaine. *Frank Lloyd Wright Home and Studio, Oak Park*. Stuttgart: Edition Axel Menges, 1996.

Hitchcock, Henry Russell. *In the Nature of Materials, 1887–1941: The Buildings of Frank Lloyd Wright*. New York: Duell, Sloan and Pearce, 1942. In the collection of Avery Architectural and Fine Arts Library, Columbia University, New York City.

Hoagland, Gertrude Fox. *Historical Survey of Oak Park, Illinois*. Oak Park: Oak Park Public Library, 1937.

Jacobsen, Elsie. "An Oral History Regarding the Frank Lloyd Wright Home and Studio Foundation." Interview by Christopher Farmer, 1997. Research Center of the Frank Lloyd Wright Preservation Trust.

Kalec, Donald G. *The Home and Studio of Frank Lloyd Wright in Oak Park, Illinois, 1889–1911*. Oak Park, IL: Frank Lloyd Wright Home and Studio Foundation, 1982.

Kalec, Donald G. *History of the Frank Lloyd Wright Home and Studio*. Frank Lloyd Wright Home and Studio Foundation Training, 1991. Videocasette.

Kalec, Donald G. "An Oral History Regarding the Frank Lloyd Wright Home and Studio Foundation." Interview by Zarine Weil, 1999. Research Center of the Frank Lloyd Wright Preservation Trust.

Lesniak, Jack. "An Oral History Regarding the Frank Lloyd Wright Home and Studio Foundation." Interview by Zarine Weil, 1999. Research Center of the Frank Lloyd Wright Preservation Trust.

Marohn, Ann. "An Oral History Regarding the Frank Lloyd Wright Home and Studio Foundation." Interview by Zarine Weil, 1999. Research Center of the Frank Lloyd Wright Preservation Trust.

Master Plan Conference. Audiotapes of the Master Plan Conference of the Frank Lloyd Wright Home and Studio Foundation, October 31, 1977.

Object File for Accession 1981.08 (Bed in girls' bedroom). Research Center of the Frank Lloyd Wright Preservation Trust.

Object File for Accession 1984.06 (Chairs in Home study). Research Center of the Frank Lloyd Wright Preservation Trust.

"Our Mess Means Progress." *Wright Angles* (January–March 1983):1–2.

Pierre, Dorathi Block, ed. *Memoirs of an American Artist: Sculptor Richard W. Bock*. Los Angeles: C. C. Publishing, 1989.

Replogle, Art. "An Oral History Regarding the Frank Lloyd Wright Home and Studio Foundation." Interview by Christopher Farmer, 1997. Research Center of the Frank Lloyd Wright Preservation Trust.

Restoration Committee of the Frank Lloyd Wright Home and Studio Foundation. *The Plan for Restoration and Adaptive Use of the Frank Lloyd Wright Home and Studio.* Chicago: University of Chicago Press, 1978.

Restoration Files. Research Center of the Frank Lloyd Wright Preservation Trust.

"Restoration Progresses." *Wright Angles* (October–December 1984):1.

Reynolds, Pam. "The Studio: Restoring Wright's Workplace." *Wright Angles* (October 1981):2–3.

Reynolds, Pam. "Studio Exterior Takes On Its 1909 Look." *Wright Angles* (January–March 1984):1–2.

Schumann, Dawn Goshorn. Speech to Department of Interior Appropriations Subcommittee. Research Center of the Frank Lloyd Wright Preservation Trust. 1976.

Schumann, Dawn Goshorn. "An Oral History Regarding the Frank Lloyd Wright Home and Studio Foundation." Interview by Zarine Weil, 1999. Research Center of the Frank Lloyd Wright Preservation Trust.

Shepard, Lyman. "An Oral History Regarding the Frank Lloyd Wright Home and Studio Foundation." Interview by Christopher Farmer, 1997. Research Center of the Frank Lloyd Wright Preservation Trust.

Smith, Nancy K. Morris, ed. "Letters, 1903–1906, by Charles E. White, Jr. from the Studio of Frank Lloyd Wright." *Journal of Architectural Education* 25 (Fall 1971):104–6.

Spencer, Robert C. Jr. "The Work of Frank Lloyd Wright." *Architectural Review VII* (June 1900):61–72.

Storrer, William Allin. *The Architecture of Frank Lloyd Wright.* Cambridge, MA: MIT Press, 1984.

"Studio Interiors Nearing Completion." *Wright Angles* (January 1985):5.

Sweeney, Karen A. *Resolving the Conflicts Involved in Integrating Climate Control System into a Historic House Museum: A Case Study, the Frank Lloyd Wright Home and Studio, Oak Park, Illinois.* July 12, 1991. Research Center of the Frank Lloyd Wright Preservation Trust.

Sweeney, Robert L. *Frank Lloyd Wright: An Annotated Bibliography.* Los Angeles: Hennessey and Ingalls, Inc., 1978.

"Things Were Different Then." *Wright Angles* (August 1984):5.

Thorpe, John G. "An Oral History Regarding the Frank Lloyd Wright Home and Studio Foundation." Interview by Christopher Farmer, 1997. Research Center of the Frank Lloyd Wright Preservation Trust.

Thorpe, John G. *The Restoration of the Home and Studio.* Frank Lloyd Wright Home and Studio Foundation Training, 1998. Videocassette.

Volunteer Manual. Oak Park, IL: Frank Lloyd Wright Home and Studio Foundation. 1998.

Wieting, Wes. "An Oral History Regarding the Frank Lloyd Wright Home and Studio Foundation." Interview by Christopher Farmer, 1997. Research Center of the Frank Lloyd Wright Preservation Trust.

Wright, Frank Lloyd. *Frank Lloyd Wright: Ausgeführte Bauten.* Berlin: Verlegt bei Ernst Wasmuth A. G., 1911.

Wright, Frank Lloyd. "In the Cause of Architecture." In *Frank Lloyd Wright: Selected Writings 1894–1940,* Frederick Gutheim, ed. New York: Duell, Sloan and Pearce, 1941.

Wright, Frank Lloyd. "Organic Architecture." In *Frank Lloyd Wright: Selected Writings 1894–1940,* Frederick Gutheim, ed. New York: Duell, Sloan and Pearce, 1941. Originally published in *Architects' Journal* (August 1936).

Wright, Frank Lloyd. *An Autobiography.* New York: Duell, Sloan and Pearce, 1943.

Wright, Frank Lloyd. *A Testament.* New York: Horizon Press, 1957.

Wright, Frank Lloyd. *Studies and Executed Buildings of Frank Lloyd Wright (Ausgeführte Bauten und Entwürfe von Frank Lloyd Wright, 1910).* Palos Park, IL: Prairie School Press, 1975.

Wright, Frank Lloyd. "Ausgeführte Bauten und Entwürfe von Frank Lloyd Wright." In *Frank Lloyd Wright Collected Writings,* Bruce Brooks Pfeiffer, ed. Vol 1. New York: Rizzoli International Publications Inc., 1992.

Wright, Frank Lloyd. *Frank Lloyd Wright Collected Writings,* Bruce Brooks Pfeiffer, ed. Vol 1. New York: Rizzoli International Publications Inc., 1992.

Wright, Frank Lloyd Jr. Interview by Donald Kalec, 1976. Research Center of the Frank Lloyd Wright Preservation Trust.

Wright, Frank Lloyd Jr. Letter to Donald Kalec, May 10, 1977.

Wright, John Lloyd. *My Father Who Is on Earth.* Carbondale: Southern Illinois University Press, 1994.

Zak, Peg. "An Oral History Regarding the Frank Lloyd Wright Home and Studio Foundation." Interview by Christopher Farmer, 1997. Research Center of the Frank Lloyd Wright Preservation Trust.